Edinburgh

Edinburgh

ALLAN MASSIE

First published in Great Britain in 1994
by Sinclair-Stevenson
an imprint of Reed Consumer Books Ltd
Michelin House, 81 Fulham Road, London sw3 6rb
and Auckland, Melbourne, Singapore and Toronto

A CIP catalogue record for this book
is available at the British Library
isbn 1 85619 244 x (hardback)
isbn 1 85619 556 2 (paperback)

Typeset by Deltatype Ltd, Ellesmere Port, Cheshire
Printed and bound in Great Britain
by The Bath Press Ltd

for
Patti and Lindsay
with love

Contents

List of Illustrations

Illustrations in colour are shown by *

Prologue

1 Origins

2 Royal Edinburgh

9 The Underside of Things

10 Victorian Edinburgh

11 Stevenson and Edinburgh

12 The Years to 1914

13 Between the Wars

Prologue

On the afternoon of 9 November 1809 Thomas Carlyle arrived in Edinburgh for the first time. He had walked twenty miles that

Thomas Carlyle
by Thomas Woolner

day, a third of his journey from his home in Annandale. He was fifteen and about to enrol at the University. That the son of a stonemason should do so was a mark of the difference between

Scotland and England, where the two Universities were almost entirely reserved for the sons of gentlemen and the well-to-do; Scotland was the land of 'the Democratic Intellect'. It was intended that Carlyle should eventually train for the ministry. He arrived homesick and weary, this 'chequering the mysterious hopes and forecastings of what Edinburgh and the Student element would be'.

His companion, a second-year student, anxious to impress, led him, after they had established themselves in lodgings in 'Simon Square, the poor locality', to Parliament House and 'dragged me in with him to a scene which I have never forgotten'.

An immense Hall, dimly lighted from the top of the walls, and perhaps with candles burning in it here and there; all in strange *chiaroscuro*, and filled with what I thought (exaggeratively), a thousand or two of human creatures; all astir in a boundless buzz of talk, and simmering about in every direction, some solitary, some in groups. By degrees I noticed that some were in wig and black gown, some not, but in common clothes, all well-dressed; that here and there on the sides of the Hall, were little thrones with enclosures, and steps leading up; red-velvet figures sitting in said thrones, and the black-gowned eagerly speaking to them – Advocates, pleading to Judges, as I easily understood. How they could be heard in such a grinding din was somewhat a mystery. Higher up on the walls, stuck there like swallows in their nests, sat other humbler figures; these I found were the sources of certain wildly plangent lamentable sounds or echoes which from time to time pierced the universal noise of feet and voices, and rose unintelligibly about it, as if in the bitterness of incurable woe; – Cries of the Court, I gradually came to understand. And this was Themis in her Outer House;

such a scene of chaotic din and hurlyburly as I had never figured before. It seems to me there were four or five times as many people in that Outer House as there now usually are; and doubtless there is something of fact in this, such have been the curtailments and abatements of Law Practice in the Head Courts since then, and transference of it to the County jurisdictions.

His guide, one Smail, 'a very innocent conceited, insignificant but strict-minded orthodox creature', had done well to lead him there that first afternoon in Edinburgh, for Parliament House was then, in that late summer of the Scottish Enlightenment, the focal point of the city's, and indeed the nation's, intellectual life; as it had been indeed since the Treaty of Union brought Scotland's independent Parliament to an end, and left the building to the lawyers. The General Assembly of the Church of Scotland, that other great institution left untouched by Union, would meet in Edinburgh every year; but that was only for one week in early summer (a week when, it was said, the city's brothels did their best trade). The Law was different: a perpetual presence, despite the Courts' long vacations; and the great men of Edinburgh were its lawyers: the Senators of the College of Justice and the Advocates in Parliament House, the Writers to the Signet who were, among other things, the nobility's and gentry's men of business or 'doers', so that it was claimed that not an acre of land was sold in Scotland but an Edinburgh lawyer got his cut.

In his *Reminiscences*, written in old age, Carlyle reflected that there were doubtless 'notable figures, now all vanished utterly, wandering about as part of that continual hurlyburly . . . Great Law Lords This and That, great Advocates *alors célèbres* (as Thiers

Edinburgh from the Crown of St Giles
attributed to Robert Barker: Edinburgh at the time of Carlyle's first visit

has it): Cranstouns, Cockburn, Jeffrey, Walter Scott, John Clerk . . . ,' but the only one he clearly remembered was Clerk, 'there veritably hitching about, whose strong grim countenance with its black far-projecting brows and look of great sagacity fixed him in my memory'. It was the general scene which had so deeply impressed him: the animation, the bustle, the sense of something important being driven forward amidst the confusion.

Later however he would reflect that he 'rather dimly felt there was something trivial, doubtful, and not quite of the highest type, in our Edinburgh admiration for the great Lights and Law Sages . . .' This contributed to his disenchantment with Edinburgh. Carlyle is a key figure in its history, even though he lived there only a few years, first as a student, subsequently as a hack journalist in the then suburb of Comely Bank. For Carlyle arrived when Edinburgh could lay claim to being, as it styled itself, 'the Athens of the North'. In the previous half-century it had been home at times to David Hume, Adam Smith and Walter Scott – the greatest philosopher, the deepest thinker on matters social and economic, the most prodigious novelist, in Europe. It could boast the finest University and the most advanced medical science in Britain. It was said that a man could stand by the Mercat Cross and 'in a few minutes, take fifty men of genius by the hand'. Jeffrey's *Edinburgh Review* was the arbiter of taste. Edinburgh might no longer be the capital of an independent kingdom, but it was truly the alternative capital of the United Kingdom.

Carlyle was the first man of outstanding talent in the generation that succeeded Scott's; and he found Edinburgh insufficient to nurture his genius. After a few years on a farm in Dumfriesshire, he removed to London. The city would continue to expand and enrich itself; it would still produce men of genius, especially in the physical sciences, but it would never recapture the lustre of the Enlightenment.

The story of Edinburgh is therefore a record of the city's rise and decline. When Carlyle last visited Parliament House and surveyed the Outer Hall, 'it seemed like a place fallen asleep, fallen almost dead'.

1

Origins

Edinburgh is not old in comparison with the cities of Greece or Italy, even with London and Paris. There is no evidence of Roman occupation, and the first reference to dwellers in the Forth Valley comes from Ptolemy's *Geography* of AD 160. An early chronicler of Scottish history, Andrew of Wyntoun, claimed admittedly that a king called Ebrawce, said to have had more than fifty children from some twenty wives, had built a 'Maiden's castle' there a thousand years earlier, and 'bygged Edynburghe wyth-alle', but this may be received with scepticism. At some point in Roman or post-Roman times, the Castle Rock was occupied by the Celtic tribe called the Gododdin, who gave it the name Dunedin, 'fortress of the hill slope'. Later, around 638, the south of Scotland was subjugated by Edwin, King of Northumbria, an Angle or Saxon: the anglicised version of the name dates from this period, but it is a mistake to think of it as Edwin's Burgh.

In the middle of the tenth century, the Kings of Scots expelled the Northumbrian rulers and established the frontier more or less where it is today, though the exact line between England and Scotland would shift repeatedly throughout the Middle Ages. Malcolm Canmore (Malcolm III, the young prince of Shakespeare's *Macbeth*) built what is described as a hunting lodge on the Castle Rock, though his main residence was safely on the other side of the Forth at Dunfermline. However his queen, the Saxon princess Margaret, who is usually credited with (or blamed for) taking the first steps in the long struggle which gradually pushed back Gaelic culture and led to the extinction of the Celtic Church and Scotland's full incorporation into European

Christendom, built a chapel on the rock. This survives, and is the oldest building in Edinburgh.

She died in the hunting lodge or castle, with a display of exemplary piety, on receiving news of her husband's death in battle near Alnwick. Her sons were then besieged in the castle by the king's brother Donald Bane, who is usually taken as being representative of the Celtic interest. According to the historian

St Margaret's Chapel, Edinburgh Castle

John of Fordun (writing several centuries later), they escaped, taking the queen's body with them, by a postern on the western side of the rock. 'Some, indeed, tell us that, during the whole of this journey, a cloudy mist was round about all this family, and miraculously sheltered them from the gaze of any of their foes . . .'

Since Margaret was to be canonised, this is all quite appropriate and indeed almost to be expected; those who know Edinburgh will also be aware that mists, known as 'haars', are frequent enough not to be thought 'miraculous'. Edinburgh has, in the opinion of Robert Louis Stevenson, 'one of the vilest climates under heaven. She is liable to be beaten upon by all the winds that blow, to be drenched with rain, to be buried in cold sea fogs out of the east, and powdered with snow as it comes flying southward from the Highland hills. The weather is raw and boisterous in winter, shifty and ungenial in summer, and a downright necrological purgatory in the spring.'

All Margaret's sons became in succession Kings of Scots, and the youngest, David, has a special place in Edinburgh's history, because he founded the Abbey of Holyrood for Augustinian canons in 1128. They in turn gave its name to the Canongate, the lower part of the Royal Mile; separated from Edinburgh proper in medieval times by the gate of the Netherbow, the Canongate remained an independent burgh till 1856. The Church of St Giles, which became 'the High Kirk of Edinburgh', was founded about the same time.

Medieval Edinburgh crept down the spine of the Castle Rock. It was not yet the capital of Scotland and did not indeed formally become so till 1633, but it was already a frequent royal residence. The Kings of Scots were, like all medieval monarchs, peripatetic, partly because this was the only way in which they could maintain a semblance of law, partly because it was easier to bring the court to food stores than food stores to the court. Edinburgh did not receive a royal charter till Robert the Bruce gave it one in 1329; there are many more ancient burghs in Scotland. It was by then, however, beginning to assume the pattern that still distinguishes the Old Town, as houses straggled down from the castle and up the hill from the abbey. Although

very little in the way of medieval building survives in Edinburgh, the Old Town retains the sense of a medieval city. Defoe thought it presented 'the effect of one vast castle'. It still looks like a city on guard. Compared with Lucca or Rouen, Durham or Cologne, Edinburgh is sadly deficient in medieval architecture; yet, in its operatic style, it recalls the Middle Ages more intensely than any of them.

The deception is carried further. The castle looks impregnable. It has been repeatedly captured. Indeed, Robert the Bruce was so impressed by the ease with which it was retaken by his nephew Thomas Randolph, Earl of Moray, that he demolished it, except for St Margaret's Chapel. By the end of the fourteenth century it had been rebuilt, though it is one of the curiosities of history that much of its fortification was the work of English armies; they found it more useful as a means of controlling the Lothians than the Scots found it an effective defence in time of invasion. Edward III, who built Windsor Castle, enlarged the enclosed area, and the fortification of Edinburgh resembled Windsor in several respects.

It has the air of a place of great strategic importance, but in reality Edinburgh was always open to attack from the south and could in any case be bypassed without risk. Consequently, few great battles were fought in its immediate vicinity. In strategic terms it cannot be compared to Stirling which, commanding the only possible passage of the Forth for a medieval army, secures the route from north to south. It was therefore the neighbourhood of Stirling that saw the great battles of the Wars of Independence: Stirling Bridge, Falkirk and Bannockburn.

But if the town, unprotected for most of its history by the enclosing wall characteristic of medieval cities, could be easily entered, and if the castle was less formidable than it seems, any army might nevertheless run into difficulties on account of the nature of the place. That was the experience of the Earl of Hertford's forces in 1544. They found themselves trapped in the narrow defiles of the closes and wynds that ran off the High Street and Lawnmarket. Edinburgh might indeed have been designed (but of course it was in no sense designed) for defensive street-fighting. It was the configuration of the city that later made

A Street in Old Edinburgh
by Henry Duguid

the Edinburgh mob so formidable. It could surge out from the rabbit warren of the high buildings, dark closes and darker cellars, do its work, then retreat into invisibility.

Bruce's charter gave Edinburgh status. Even more important for its future was Scotland's loss of Berwick, which, situated at the mouth of the Tweed, had been the country's greatest port and its natural gateway to the Continent. Berwick was first taken by the English in 1292 (Bruce's queen was later imprisoned there and the Countess of Buchan, who had crowned him king, was suspended in a cage from its castle walls). Though recaptured by Bruce, it fell to the English again in the 1330s, and thereafter changed hands several times in the course of the next century and a half. This left Edinburgh and its port of Leith with no serious trading rival between the English border and the Firth of Tay. As a result by 1500 it paid 60 per cent of all customs duties levied by the Crown. It dominated Scotland's trade in wool (from the Border valleys) and hides from the Lothians and the Merse; it exported more than half the coal sent forth from Scotland. 'By 1600 Edinburgh together with its port of Leith was the undisputed entrepôt for the great bulk of Scottish trade.'*

By 1500 there were fourteen distinct markets in Edinburgh. Cattle and sheep were herded into the city along the Cowgate, first mentioned in the 1320s and running parallel to the Canongate and High Street, but at a lower level, to be slaughtered and butchered in the neighbourhood of the Grassmarket. In 1499 Edinburgh exported more than 40,000 sheepskins and 24,000 hides. A hundred years later the total had multiplied several times over. There was a textile trade too, and a trade in grain. In the medieval period brewing was an occupation reserved to the wives of burgesses: 288 female brewers were recorded early in the sixteenth century. The founding of the Society of Brewers in 1598 changed this. Brewing became a capitalist enterprise. It has remained one of Edinburgh's chief industries, its agreeable smell pervading most quarters of the city.

Crowded, insanitary, plague-ridden, Edinburgh was like most medieval cities: no filthier or more unhealthy than others, and no better either.

* Lynch, *History of Scotland.*

Medieval Edinburgh was also an ecclesiastical city. Apart from the Abbey of Holyrood, the Dominicans (Blackfriars) and Franciscans (Greyfriars) had houses with large gardens south of the Cowgate. Even today the name of the district of Sciennes around the University recalls the Convent of St Catherine of Siena. The Collegiate Church of St Mary's in the Fields (Kirk o' Fields) lay between the Dominican and Franciscan houses. All these monastic and collegiate buildings were destroyed and sacked at the time of the Reformation, and the district stood unpopulated and more or less abandoned for a couple of decades. In 1582, however, the Townis College (the University) was built from the ruined splendour of St Mary's in the Fields, the High School was established where the Blackfriars had worshipped, and Greyfriars became the city's second parish church, almost certainly using any part of the old building which had survived looting. The Royal Infirmary, Surgeon's Hall, George Heriot's Hospital and School, and the Merchant Maiden School, would all be built in the seventeenth century on what had been the property of the religious orders.

Holyrood Abbey
('The Abby Church of Holyrood-House').
The nave and northwest tower in the 17th century

We can catch something of the flavour of late medieval Edinburgh in the work of Scotland's greatest poet, William Dunbar. We know little of his life and are fortunate to have his work. A small collection was published in 1508 by Scotland's first printers, Chapman and Myllar, licensed by James IV only two years previously; but other poems were found only in manuscript collections and the first full edition did not appear till 1834.

Sculpted frieze of angels above west door of Holyrood Abbey, early 13th century

Dunbar seems to have been born in East Lothian about 1460, and he almost certainly studied at St Andrews. He may have been a Franciscan novice who later took priest's orders. He served on various embassies to France and England, the latter to arrange the marriage of James IV to Margaret Tudor, which he celebrated in *The Thrissel and the Rose*. It is probable that he spent much of his adult life in Edinburgh and it is clear that he knew the city well.

He deplored, as poets have subsequently, the close-fisted attitudes of the City Fathers:

> Quhy will ye merchants of renoun,
> Lat Edinburgh, your nobil toun
> For lak of reformatioun
> 　　The commone profeitt tyine and fame

Think ye not schame,
That onie uther regioun
Sall with dishonour hurt your name?

May nane pass throw your principall gaittis
For stink of haddockis and of scattis,
For cryis of carlinges and debaittis,
For fensum flytingis of defamis,
　Think ye not schame
Before strangeris of all estaittis
That sic dishonour hurt your name?

Dunbar was the first great poet to hold up a mirror to Edinburgh, and to emphasise what has become a conventional contrast between wealth and dignity on the one hand and poverty and vice on the other. He has a remarkable range of language, from the most ornate to demotic vulgarity. Here, too, he serves as a precursor, even model, for later writers about the city. His command of invective is unparalleled, though no doubt the Newhaven fishwives ran him close. All the same, it is only from a vibrant literary culture that verses like his flyting of Walter Kennedy could come:

Conspiratour, cursit cocatrice, hell caa,
　Turk, trompour, traitour, tyran intemperate;
Thou irefull attircop, Pilote apostata,
Judas, jow, juglour, Lollard laureate;
Sarazene, symonyte provit, Pagan pronunciate,
machomete, manesuourne, bugrist abominable,
Devill, dampnit dog, sodomyte insatiable,
With Gog and Magog grete glorificate.

Dunbar was no lone voice. Edinburgh abounded in poets. Gavin Douglas, a little younger than Dunbar, translated Virgil's *Aeneid* into Scots. The Prologue to Book VII offers a vividly recognisable picture of winter in Edinburgh:

The law valle flodderit all with spait,
The plane stretis and every hie way
Full of floschis, dubbis, myre and clay.

Douglas, a son of the Earl of Angus and a Provost of St Giles, later
Bishop of Dunkeld, had a palace in Edinburgh and was made a
freeman of the city a few weeks after Flodden. Nevertheless he
was imprisoned by the regent Albany a couple of years later in
what he called 'the wyndy and richt unpleasant castell and royk
of Edinburgh'.

   Another poet was Sir David Lyndsay of the Mount, author of
the play *The Thrie Estaitis*, a satire on the pre-Reformation Church
which, after four centuries of neglect, was to be gloriously
revived by Tyrone Guthrie at the first of the Edinburgh Festivals.

Sir David Lyndsay of the Mount
(anon.)

If Lyndsay had known how the reformed religion would suppress the drama, he might have sung a different note. The City
Fathers took a dim view of merriment, an attitude they were to
maintain almost to the present day. After the Reformation, they
clamped down on the May Day celebrations presided over by a
Lord of Misrule, who went by the name of Robin Hood – so
widespread was that myth – and ordered the expulsion of 'all
menstrallis, pyperis, fidleris, common sangsteris, and specially
of badrie and filthie sangs, and sicklyke all vagabonds and

maisterless persons what hes na service nor honest industrie to leif be'.

The Reformation and the sixteenth century would therefore see the opening of a long engagement which has never been wholly abandoned, as Edinburgh learned to wear a double face, to preach virtue in a cold and sober manner, while all the time, in subterranean dens and occasionally in the dark streets, that species of virtue was mocked and defied.

2

Royal Edinburgh

It was under the Stewart kings, then, that Edinburgh began to assume importance, and the second Stewart, Robert III (1390–1406), granted a new charter permitting the burghers to build houses within the castle walls and to pass freely in and out without paying tolls. Nevertheless, though Parliament might meet there, and laws be enacted there, and justice be administered there, the kings still preferred to burden the monks of Holyrood with their presence rather than take up residence in the castle itself. The abbey was not of course defensible, and when Henry IV of England invaded Scotland, more or less unmolested, the monks petitioned him to spare their abbey. He replied, 'Far be it from me to be so inhuman as to harm any holy house, especially Holyrood in which my father [John of Gaunt] once found a safe refuge . . . Besides I am myself half Scots by the blood of the Comyns.' It is no wonder that the sixteenth-century historian Hector Boece described this English invader as 'a pleasant enemy'.

Gradually the castle grew, though it could never have been either a comfortable or even a spacious residence: the room shown to tourists as that in which Mary Queen of Scots gave birth to her son, the future James VI and I, is scarcely more than a cupboard. Mrs Oliphant, the nineteenth-century novelist and historian, observed that it 'would scarcely be occupied, save under protest, by a housemaid in our days'.

Fifteen-century Scotland was turbulent, but the same could be said of England and France as well. All three countries show the same pattern: of a monarchy struggling to control a nobility

Queen Mary's room in Edinburgh Castle (anon.)

whose members were petty princes in their own localities, capable of raising private armies. In all three countries factions among the nobility vied at times to secure control of the king, the fount of justice, honour and authority. Only at certain moments throughout the century could a strong king – Henry V or Edward

IV in England, Louis XI in France, the Jameses in Scotland, but only for brief periods in each reign – consider himself master of his kingdom.

In England the turbulence was made worse by the failure of the French war and a disputed succession to the throne; in France by the attempts of the Dukes of Burgundy to establish themselves as independent princes; in Scotland by a sequence of minorities during which the regency was disputed as nobles fought to secure the person of the boy king. James I spent the first eighteen years of his reign in captivity in England. James II was six when his father was murdered in Blackfriars Abbey in Perth. James III was only two years older when his father was killed by an exploding cannon at the siege of Roxburgh Castle in 1460, James V eighteen months old when his father fell at Flodden, Mary of Scots only six days old when James turned his face to the wall and died, it was said, of grief, 'in despair', according to the chronicler Lyndsay of Pitscottie, 'that he could nevir recover his honour agane'. No wonder there was no smooth or regular development of the kingdom. At a time when kings really governed, only one in a century and a half, James IV, did not require a regent; and he had been a party to the rebellion which resulted in the murder of his father after the battle of Sauchieburn in 1488.

Violence was then characteristic of Scottish political life, but not unique to Scotland. In France Orléanists and Burgundians engaged in murder and revengeful murder from that November night in the black winter of 1407 – frost endured for sixty-six days on end – when Louis, Duke of Orléans, was cut down in a Paris street on his way from supper with the queen. In England the struggles between York and Lancaster made the block a frequent end to a political career. Edinburgh Castle saw its own horrors, though they can scarcely compare with the murders, both secret and judicial, perpetrated in the Tower of London.

James II, as a boy of ten, was witness to one of the most horrid killings in 1440. The regency was then divided between two lords, Sir Alexander Livingstone, the Keeper of Stirling Castle, and Sir William Crichton, the Custodian of Edinburgh. Both feared the power of the great Border house of Douglas, whose head, William, the sixth earl, a youth of spirit and ambition, seemed to threaten the two Keepers' position. Livingstone and Crichton laid their rivalry aside in the face of this danger. They made friendly approaches to the young earl and eventually persuaded him to be the king's guest in Edinburgh Castle. He arrived there with his younger brother David, a friend, Malcolm Fleming of Cumbernauld, and a host of armed retainers. These, however, were lodged outside the castle.

The traditional version of what followed is given by Sir Walter Scott in *Tales of a Grandfather*:

> Of a sudden the scene began to change. At an entertainment which was served up to the Earl and his brother, the head of a black bull was placed on the table. The Douglases knew this, according to a custom which prevailed in Scotland, to be the sign of death, and leaped from the table in great dismay. But they were seized by armed men who entered the apartment. They underwent a mock trial, in which all the insolences of their ancestors were charged against them, and were condemned to immediate execution. The young King wept and implored Livingstone and Crichton to show mercy to the young noblemen, but in vain. These cruel men only reproved him for weeping at the death of those whom they called his enemies. The brothers were led out to the court of the castle, and beheaded without delay. Malcolm Fleming of Cumbernauld, a faithful adherent of their house, shared the same fate.

The young king learned the lesson well: politics is about power. A few years later he stabbed the eighth Earl of Douglas to death in Stirling Castle. That murder was approved by a Parliament summoned for that purpose, but the earlier murder of the two brothers was long remembered and commemorated in rhyme:

> Edinburgh castle, towne and toure,
> God grant thou sink for sinne!
> And that even for the black dinner
> Erl Douglas gat therein.

Edinburgh saw more violence, confused and usually inconclusive, in the reign of his son, James III. There was first the usual struggle over the regency, this time disputed by the boy king's mother, Mary of Gueldres, and James Kennedy, Bishop of St Andrews, himself a grandson of Robert III. Mary persuaded the first Parliament of the reign, meeting in the castle where she herself was resident – while Kennedy, in possession of the king, was lurking at the bottom of the hill in the abbey – to name her regent, a measure which the bishop then tried to bully the Estates into rescinding. This provoked a tumult in the streets, though which side the people of Edinburgh supported is impossible to tell. But it set the pattern for many subsequent riots, and is notable as the first recorded stirring of the Edinburgh mob which was to be so formidable and often so disturbingly well organised.

None of the Stewart kings is easy to assess, partly of course because of the paucity of evidence, but this has not prevented historians from indulging in psychological analyses. There is this justification for the enterprise: that each appears to have been a man of complex personality who puzzled his contemporaries. James III has been called the most gifted and the most unpleasant of them. We have no means of knowing whether this is true, but it is clear that he was the least-suited of the Jameses to the requirements of late medieval kingship. He was neither industrious nor consistently strong-minded; he preferred the arts to war, and the company of architects, musicians and artists to that of his proud and probably illiterate nobility. He failed to enforce the law strictly, and he thought Scotland should live at peace with England.

He had a greater misfortune than his character however: two brothers, the Duke of Albany and the Earl of Mar, who would seem to have been more in tune with the general temper of the Scots nobility, or could at least serve as a rallying point to all those who disapproved of the king. Not surprisingly James was wary of his brothers, and not surprisingly he found people ready to fan his fears. His Flemish astrologer warned him that his chief danger arose from his own family, and this warning is said to have been confirmed by certain witches whom the king consulted. He may have had more concrete reason for suspicion. At any rate he arrested both his brothers. The younger, John, Earl of Mar, was imprisoned in the Canongate Tolbooth where he died – bled to death, it is said, in his bath (bathing was fashionable in the fifteenth century among those who could afford it: the Lord Treasurer's accounts for 1474 record the purchase of broadcloth 'to cover a bath-tub for the Queen' and 'for a sheet to put about the Queen in the bath-tub').

The other brother, Albany, was imprisoned in Edinburgh Castle (where the king himself was resident), but escaped by a stratagem which bears a very close resemblance to that employed by the Duc de Beaufort in Dumas' novel *Twenty Years After*. A French ship having arrived at Leith with a cargo of wine, Albany received a message that a passage would be available on the return journey. He therefore sent to the port for wine, and invited the Captain of the Guard to sup with him. The wine was drugged, the captain and the other guards passed out; their sleep was made permanent by the dagger, and Albany and his servant escaped down the north side of the Castle Rock. The servant broke his hip in the descent, but Albany is reported to have carried him to Leith. In the morning the watchman discovered a rope dangling from the castle wall 'and when they missed the Duke of Albany and his chamber chylde, they ran speedily and shewed the king how the matter had happened. But he would not give it credence till he passed himself and saw the matter.'

Three years later the king himself would be in effect a prisoner in his own castle. His rule had outraged his nobles, who were especially offended by his friendship for the architect Cochrane, whom he had created Earl of Mar, and others of low degree. (Since Cochrane was responsible for that masterpiece of Scots Renaissance architecture, the Great Hall of Stirling Castle, the king's taste seems more admirable than his contemporaries thought.) The opportunity for revenge came when James summoned an army to resist an English invasion intended to put the exiled Albany on the throne as a vassal of the King of England. The discontented nobles came together in the parish church of Lauder, where they resolved to get rid of the low-born favourites, and argued whether they should depose the king at the same time. Deciding against this extreme course, they contented themselves with compelling him to watch the hanging of his friends from the bridge at Lauder. He was then conveyed back to Edinburgh, apparently with all outward marks of respect, and lodged in the castle, king in name but for the time being powerless, and embittered by the insults he had received and the murders he had been forced to witness.

Meanwhile the English army advanced, led by Richard, Duke of Gloucester (the future Richard III), with Albany at his right hand. Albany and Gloucester entered the Tolbooth where the chief lords were sitting in council and demanded that the king be set free. It is all very confused, for Albany's agreement with England seems to be contradicted by what happened. One can only assume that he thought he might exercise power more safely through his brother, and that he realised that James retained enough support to make any usurpation dangerous. Certainly it would seem that the burghers of Edinburgh favoured the king. They were perhaps less offended by his taste for the humbly born than the nobles were. At any rate, when he was free, he rewarded the city with a new charter which guaranteed the independence of its municipality, granted it the right to levy customs at the port of Leith, and, as a sign of these privileges, presented it with a banner called the Blue Blanket to be displayed on all solemn public occasions.

If poor James III was to be judged an inadequate king, his son James IV was seen as the very pattern of the Renaissance prince. He was as enthusiastic a builder as his father, but in his case this was excused because he was a warrior also and an energetic administrator. In Edinburgh he left his mark chiefly on Holyrood. James was in Pitscottie's words 'gritumly given to bigging of palaces', and the monks who owned Holyrood were displaced by the royal household and found themselves restricted to the church, cloister and some adjoining rooms. By the time he married Margaret Tudor in 1503 James had furnished himself with a substantial palace with gallery and entrance wing. His son James V carried on the work, adding a tower in the French style to the north and planning another to the south, though this was not built till Sir William Bruce remodelled the palace in the reign of Charles II. The façade of James's palace was composed of stone-mullioned flat windows and projecting bow-fronted ones.

Unfortunately the palace on which James embarked was never finished. It suffered moreover from the ravages of war, and

The Palace of Holyroodhouse by James Gordon of Rothiemay, 1647

so Scotland was robbed of what might have been a masterpiece of Northern Renaissance architecture. Holyrood was sacked by Hertford in 1544 and again in 1547, in that brutal attempt by Henry VIII to bully the Scots into agreeing to the marriage of their infant queen to his son Prince Edward. Hertford's methods were considered by the Scots to be too rough a wooing; they also cost us the beautiful abbeys of Melrose, Dryburgh, Kelso and Jedburgh, all burned by the invader. Mary in her brief reign in Scotland began to repair the damage to Holyrood, and further improvements, or restorations, were effected for the coronation of Charles I in 1633, but it was burnt again by Cromwell's troopers after the Battle of Dunbar in 1650; so that Holyroodhouse as it stands today is essentially the building which Sir William Bruce constructed for Charles II's minister, the Duke of Lauderdale.

Nevertheless the building is more associated in popular repute with Mary Queen of Scots than with any other monarch. This is true of the city itself, for some of the most dramatic episodes in that career which has made her the subject of so many novels, plays, operas and films as well as biographies were enacted there.

Mary, Queen of Scots
after François Clouet

She was only nineteen and already the widowed Queen of France when she returned to Scotland in August 1561. The country had been convulsed in the years of her absence and a revolution had taken place in the last two: the Church of Rome had been overthrown and monastic houses sacked and dissolved; the French alliance which had been at the centre of Scottish foreign policy for more than two and a half centuries was ended, and a new alliance made with Protestant England; indeed the leaders of the revolutionary party, the Presbyterian ministers headed by John Knox, now Minister of St Giles, and the Lords of the Congregation, among whom Mary's illegitimate half-brother the Earl of Moray was the most prominent, had received material and moral support from England, and in some cases were no better than English pensioners.

The revolution indeed had broken out in Edinburgh on St Giles's Day, 1 September, 1558. It was the custom to parade a statue of the city's tutelar saint through the streets. The queen's mother, the regent Mary of Guise, had declared her intention of participating in the ceremony herself on this occasion. Knox, in his version of the day's events, declares that this was because she feared lest 'some tumult should arise'; but it is more likely that she intended to honour the city by her presence and to fortify the threatened Faith. Someone had stolen the saint's statue – it is not difficult to guess who was responsible – but the archbishops ordered the Provost and Council either to find it or to produce another at their own expense. So they borrowed one from the Greyfriars and nailed it to a barrow; the procession took place, to the great indignation of Knox. Then the regent retired to dine, while the statue was left outside in the High Street.

Knox gives a vivid version of what happened next, which is probably true in outline, though biased in interpretation:

> And so began one to cry 'down with idol, down with it'; and so, without delay it was pulled down . . . One took him by the heels and dadding his head to the Causeway, left Dagon [a Philistine god] without head or hands and said, 'Fie upon thee, thou young St Giles, thy father would have tarried four such.' This considered, we say, the Priests and Friars fled faster than they did at Pinkie Cleuch [the battle fought at Musselburgh in 1547 where those that fled fastest were not priests or friars, but the Scots nobility, some of whom were now among the godly Lords of the Congregation]. Down go the crosses, off go the surplices, round capes, cornets with the crowns. The Greyfriars gaped, the Blackfriars blew and the priests panted and fled for such a sudden fray came never amongst the generation of Antichrist within this realm before.

IOANNES CNOXVS.

So the realm to which the young Mary returned that misty August day was disturbed indeed; and her own situation was of the utmost difficulty. She was Catholic queen of a country which had undergone a Protestant revolution. She was a woman ruler at a time when men questioned the capacity, and indeed the right, of women to rule; and Knox himself had written a pamphlet denouncing such rule as 'monstrous'. She represented the defeated French party, and, to make matters more delicate still, believed she was rightfully Queen of England also, instead of her cousin Elizabeth, to whom the ascendant party in Scotland owed their supremacy. For while it was true that the Reformation in Scotland was a popular movement, and that Knox had the support of many burghers of Edinburgh as well as of the nobility who hoped to profit from the seizure of Church lands, it is also true, though often forgotten, that the success of the Reformation was assured only by English arms and money, which many Scots were the more willing to accept because they resented the French influence which the regent had welcomed and the French troops with which she had thought to bolster her power.

Mary showed her courage from the start by insisting on the right to hear Mass in her private chapel, though the Parliament, summoned to Edinburgh and meeting in St Giles in July 1559, had abolished the Mass and declared that none should hear or say that office 'or be present thereat, under the pain of confiscation of all their goods movable and immovable, and punishing of their bodies at the discretion of the Magistrates'. Nevertheless the first Sunday that Mary was in Holyrood the Mass was said, even though her half-brother Moray had to guard the door, while a Fife laird, Lindsay of the Byres, was urging others that 'the idolatrous priests should die the death'. Knox was naturally alarmed, for he said that he feared one Mass more than ten thousand armed men, and he denounced its celebration in the royal chapel, in one of his most vehement sermons delivered in St Giles. But there were enough of the nobility and gentry who thought that the queen should not be disturbed in her worship to overrule Knox, even if it was impossible to silence him. On the narrow basis of legality, of course, the queen was in the right, for the Parliament which had abolished the Mass had not been summoned by royal

John Knox
after Adrian Vanson

command and was therefore no true Parliament at all; and in any case the sovereign could not be bound by a law to which she had not given her consent.

Knox prudently drew back. In private conversations, of which he left a long, complacent and unreliable account, he argued the matter of religion with the queen. He has, by his own lights, the better of the argument, but the unprejudiced reader of his version will think that the queen more than held her own, for against the authority of history which the Church of Rome embodied, he could in the end offer only the flat assertion that God's will was what he said it was. Whatever one thinks of the discussion itself, the keen debate between queen and prophet was of a quality rare in royal palaces, and curiously in the end one feels a certain affection for the old bigot as well as admiration for the girl's courage and intelligence.

Her loyalty to her faith was praiseworthy, for a decision to embrace the reformed religion would have alleviated her position. Even so it is easy to exaggerate the extent to which that had already conquered. Many noble families still adhered to Catholicism and even in Edinburgh only about a sixth of the burgesses took communion at Knox's reformed church. The Town Council had conformed and issued a proclamation commanding 'all monks, friars, priests and other papists and profane persons to pass forth of Edinburgh within the next twenty-four hours after halloween, under pain of burning upon the cheek and the hurling of them through the town'; but when Mary responded to this insult to her faith by dismissing the provost and the bailies and appointing people more agreeable to herself, there was no outcry. It is probable that the leading citizens were more concerned with maintaining peace and ensuring that nothing disrupted trade and business than with theological quarrels. Mary pleased them by agreeing to a petition to grant the confiscated lands of the Blackfriars to the town for a hospital for the poor. In a few years she seemed to have appeased her critics and there was even talk of a Catholic revival. It was necessary for the reformers to keep the pressure up, to use the mob to intimidate any who hoped to reverse the course of the revolution. In April 1565 a Catholic priest, formerly attached to St Giles, was discovered saying a private Mass and dragged to the Mercat Cross, where he was pelted with eggs. Zealots claimed that 100,000 were thrown, but since the population of Edinburgh then amounted only to some 12,000 or 13,000 persons, many of whom had better uses for eggs, it is doubtful whether so many breakfasts were sacrificed even in so godly a cause.

In other ways Mary failed to satisfy the citizens. Her restoration of Holyrood might be admired, all the more because she bore the cost from her private (French) resources, but her employment of French craftsmen is unlikely to have endeared her to the merchants and craft guilds who might have hoped to profit from the enterprise.

More serious was the matter of her marriage, even though, as a question of high politics, this did not directly concern the people of Edinburgh. It was assumed by all that the queen must marry, for no one thought that a woman could govern without a consort, and Mary herself never seems to have doubted the necessity. Various candidates were suggested, Elizabeth of England even impudently proposing her own discarded lover Robert Dudley, Earl of Leicester, who was only available because his wife had died in mysterious circumstances. Mary rejected this suggestion indignantly, but the choice she made was itself impolitic. Her cousin Henry Stewart, Lord Darnley, was the son of the Earl of Lennox, and had a claim, if a remote one, to both the English and Scottish thrones. It would have been a marriage likely to create difficulties, for it was bound to arouse Elizabeth's suspicions and in any case the Lennoxes had many enemies among other factions of the Scots nobility, even if Darnley had been a young man of great qualities. Unfortunately few figures in history have been awarded a more uniformly hostile press. The only quality allowed him is beauty, and it was doubtless this that attracted the queen who nursed the boy – he was five years younger than she – through an attack of measles. Her feelings may have been tender rather than amorous, for, although Mary may be a figure of Romance, she may also have been sexually cold. (During her long captivity in England, there was no hint of any sexual relationship; people fell in love with her from a distance, but not close at hand.) In any case, she was unable to hold Darnley's affections and the marriage was soon unhappy and seen as a mistake.

Darnley was assumed to represent the Catholic interest in the state. Nevertheless he joined with the Protestant Lords of the Congregation in the murder of the queen's Italian servant, David Rizzio, a Savoyard. The extent of Rizzio's influence with Mary can only be guessed; but it was rumoured that he was to supplant the Earl of Morton as Chancellor of Scotland. This is almost as improbable as the story that he was Mary's lover, but the two gave the Lords of the Congregation their excuse. As for Darnley, who had previously been on friendly terms with the victim, the report that Rizzio was opposed to granting Darnley the crown-matrimonial was enough.

Rizzio was the victim, but Mary herself was the target. Her half-brother Moray had objected to her marriage with Darnley, which would deprive him of power, and had led a rebellion, subsidised (though less generously than he had expected) by Elizabeth. It had been suppressed easily and Moray had fled to England, but now a Parliament had been summoned and its chief purpose was to declare Moray and his companions guilty of treason, and to be forfeit in life, lands and goods. This was enough. The conspiracy was hatched.

On 9 March, three days before the Parliament was to meet, the queen was taking supper quietly, for it was Lent and she was well advanced in pregnancy. Rizzio was with her. Meanwhile the palace was occupied by armed retainers of the Earls of Morton and Lindsay. A group of nobles, many at least half drunk, including Darnley, and led by Lord Ruthven, reputed to be a warlock, broke in on the queen, seized the unfortunate favourite and stabbed him to death before her eyes.

The news quickly spread, and the Provost and some leading citizens attempted to rescue Mary. Darnley assured them that she was safe, while she was in fact being threatened with being 'cut into collops' if she gave any trouble. Those nobles friendly to her who were resident in or around Holyrood had been taken by surprise and were powerless to intervene, one of them, James Hepburn, Earl of Bothwell, counting himself lucky to have escaped with his own life. Mary kept her head. She managed to

Henry Stewart, Lord Darnley
(anon.)

detach her husband from his confederates and advised him that he would be a fool to trust the likes of Morton and Ruthven. Then she made contact with the Archbishop of Glasgow and with his help was able to slip from the palace and flee towards Dunbar. Darnley accompanied her, urging a faster flight. When she reminded him of her condition, he told her they could make another child if this one was lost. On the way they encountered a troop of Bothwell's Borderers and with them as escort arrived safely at Dunbar, where the queen cooked eggs for their breakfast.

A few days later she turned to the work of pacification and reconciliation. She patched things up with Moray, who nevertheless secured a friendly reception in England for some of the murderers. Knox, who had also applauded the murder as 'the Lord's work', prudently withdrew into Ayrshire, and the queen was able to return to Edinburgh, where she received a warm welcome. On the morning of 16 June her son was born in that tiny closet in the castle.

'My Lord,' she told Darnley, 'God has given you and me a son, begotten by none but you.'

'This is the son,' she said, 'who (I hope) shall first unite the two kingdoms of Scotland and England.' In time he did so, and Edinburgh can therefore lay claim to being the birthplace of the Union of the Crowns.

Poor Mary was to learn not only the vicissitudes of fortune, but the fickleness of the Edinburgh mob. No doubt there was more than one mob, and no doubt many of those who had welcomed her on her return from Dunbar consulted their own safety and kept their houses less than a year later when she was brought back to Edinburgh after her capture by the rebels at the non-Battle of Carberry Hill outside Musselburgh, and the mob howled, 'Burn the hoor, burn the hoor'; but some of them must have been the same, and the change in temper may be accounted for in part at least by the events of Monday 10 February 1567, when Darnley was murdered.

The murder of Darnley is Edinburgh's great unsolved mystery, the subject of endless speculation, like the fate of the Princes in the Tower.

Mary had fallen ill at the back-end of the year, after a hard ride from Jedburgh to Hermitage Castle where her Warden of the Marches, Bothwell, was himself lying sick. Her convalescence was slow, not helped by the ministrations of her doctors, and during it her spirits were low. She talked of the unhappiness Darnley had brought her, and she even talked of suicide. She was in the company of her half-brother Moray and the leading Protestant moderate, Maitland of Lethington, and it may have been at their suggestion that the possibility of a divorce from Darnley was discussed. Whatever her feelings, she hesitated in case this should imperil the status of her son. But Lethington said, 'We shall find the means that your majesty shall be quit of him.'

Then Darnley in turn fell sick, probably of smallpox. Mary, who was immune to the disease since she had had it as a child in France, went to Glasgow to nurse him. The political situation was as tense as it was complicated, for there were reports of a new plot to re-establish Catholicism in Scotland in which both Darnley and his father were involved. Mary had disappointed some of her co-religionists by her moderation, which was itself dictated not only by her good sense but by her dynastic ambitions, directed towards securing her succession to the throne of England. But Darnley would be the weak link in any plot, for he could not keep a secret.

Having established her baby son at Holyrood, Mary rode back to Glasgow to move Darnley as soon as he was fit to travel. The original intention seems to have been that he should come to Craigmillar Castle, a couple of miles out of Edinburgh on the Dalkeith Road, but Darnley himself had made other arrangements to lodge at the Provost's house at Kirk o' Field. His rooms there had been prepared by Sir James Balfour, one of the many shady characters involved in the murder. Balfour was certainly no stranger to crime, for twenty years earlier he had been, along with Knox, one of the murderers of Cardinal Beaton, and like Knox had served time in the French galleys. Despite this, he was known as 'Blasphemous Balfour' and Knox described him and his brother Gilbert as 'men without God'.

Kirk o' Field (St Mary's in the Fields) stood on the ground

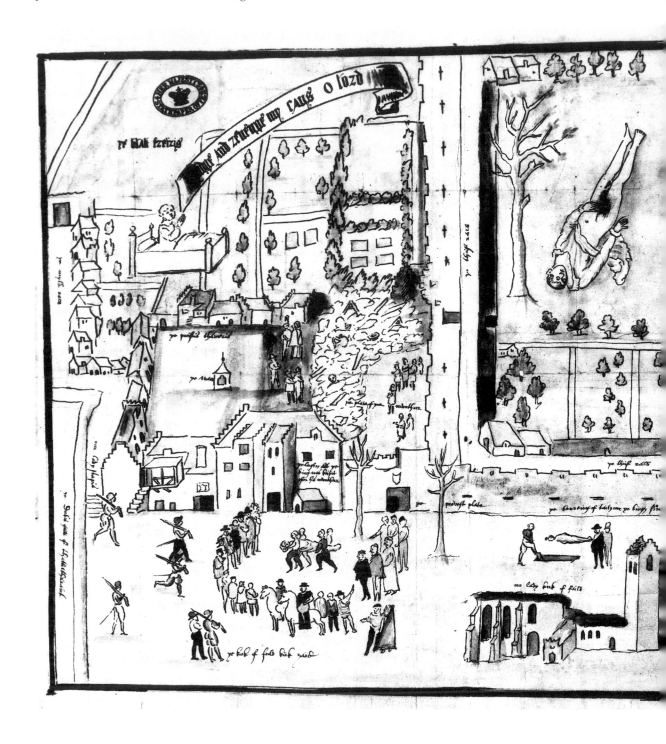

The Murder of Darnley at Kirk o' Field: contemporary drawing.
Queen Mary's infant son, the future James VI and I,
is depicted at the top left vowing revenge.

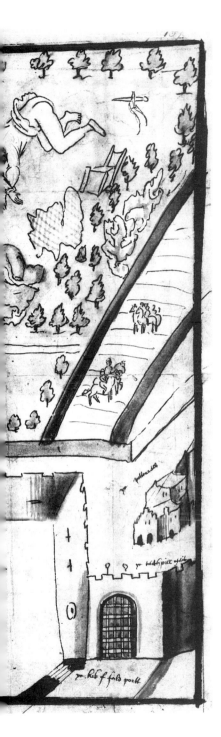

now occupied by South Bridge and the Old College of the University of Edinburgh. It was just within the Flodden Wall, and the Provost's Lodging was a large stone house set against the wall, one of a number which served as a cloister skirting the old monastic buildings. (On the other side of the wall was a disreputable lane known as 'Thief Row'.) The Presbyterian poet, historian, polemicist and liar George Buchanan, in his account of Mary's crimes, asserted that Kirk o' Field was an unsuitable residence for the convalescent king, being set at a distance from the main part of the city, amidst ruins, a place chosen, he insinuated, because any cries of alarm raised there would go unheard. But this was nonsense. It was a perfectly respectable dwelling, and anyway chosen by Darnley himself.

Mary was busy the day before her husband's death. First she attended the wedding in Holyrood of one of her French servants, Bastien, to one of her ladies-in-waiting. Later in the day there was a banquet, in James Balfour's house in the Canongate, for the new ambassador from Savoy, after which she rode to Kirk o' Field where she had promised to spend the last night of Darnley's quarantine. She sat with him for a couple of hours while he played dice with Bothwell and a number of other nobles. Then she remembered that she had promised to dance at the wedding party. Darnley objected, but was unable to prevail. On her way out of the house, she encountered one of Bothwell's servants, known as French Paris, and exclaimed, 'Jesu, Paris, how begrimed you are.' In his analysis of the Darnley murder, Eric Linklater writes, 'In all the reports of what was said, and what was heard, in that dark winter – evidence extorted from the agony of the rack or a phrase remembered in after years – nothing rings more truly than the innocent surprise of those simple, natural words.' Mary then returned to the dance at Holyrood, where she stayed only a short time. A little after midnight she had a conversation with Bothwell and the Earl of Traquair, the captain of her bodyguard. Nobody knows what was discussed.

About two in the morning of the 10th the Provost's house was shattered by an explosion which alarmed the whole city. The house was demolished; an unrecognisable body was found in the rubble. The bodies of Darnley and his valet, Taylor, were

discovered in the garden near a pear tree. There was snow on the
ground. They wore nothing but their nightshirts and the bodies
were unmarked. A kitchen chair, a quilt, a dressing gown, and
Taylor's belt and dagger were scattered around them.

What had happened? Investigation was launched. The
queen offered a free pardon for any other offences and a reward
of two thousand pounds to the first who should identify the
murderers. Bills were posted on the door of the Tolbooth, at St
Giles, the Mercat Cross, the Abbey Gate of Holyrood, and the
ports of the city, all denouncing Bothwell as the guilty man and

*James Hepburn, 4th Earl of
Bothwell*
(anon.)

naming Balfour, the servant Bastien and David Rizzio's brother
Joseph as accomplices. They also, damningly, alleged the
queen's assent. There is some evidence that these bills may have
been the work of English agents.

Bothwell was summoned to stand trial. He filled Edinburgh with armed supporters – as many as four thousand, it was claimed, though the figure is almost certainly an exaggeration. They were sufficient, however, to overawe the jury, and though the court sat for seven hours and the jury included some of Bothwell's enemies, no evidence was produced to support the indictment and he was therefore acquitted. When the queen rode to Parliament a few days later, Bothwell carried her sceptre, and when the Parliament closed on 19 April he bore the sword of honour as he escorted her back to Holyrood. The following week he abducted Mary, brought her to Dunbar Castle and raped her. They were married by Protestant rites on 14 May, and Maitland of Lethington reported that 'from her wedding day she was ever in tears and lamentation'.

After Mary's forced abdication and flight into England, the case against her and Bothwell was elaborated by the Protestant lords who feared that Elizabeth would support their queen's restoration. Evidence secured by torture enabled the Lord Justice-Clerk to produce a report which, however, defies credulity. Bothwell, he averred, had brought the gunpowder to Kirk o' Field on the night of the murder. He had first lodged it in Holyrood, and that night carried it from Blackfriars gate in saddle-bags and a trunk loaded on a grey horse; two journeys were required. This is nonsensical. The house was utterly demolished; far more of the indifferent gunpowder of the sixteenth century would have been needed than could have been brought in the way described. Moreover it defies common sense to suppose that all this could have been done that Sunday evening in Edinburgh without arousing comment. It is as certain as anything can be that the gunpowder must have been stored in the cellars of Kirk o' Field far earlier, probably before Darnley himself was brought there. The man who had the best opportunity to do this was Sir James Balfour. It should be remembered too that it was Darnley who had insisted on being lodged there rather than at Craigmillar, as Mary wished.

This supports the theory that Darnley was not the intended victim of the original plot, but rather one of its authors: that it was a Catholic plot intended to eliminate the queen and the chief

Protestant lords who would be entertained at Kirk o' Field while Darnley himself slipped away on some excuse. Darnley, however, was a blabbermouth and the Protestant lords received due warning. They may have hoped to turn it to their advantage (and indeed they were to be the chief gainers from the murder) but were forestalled by Bothwell, who discovered the gunpowder and decided to act on his own accord. If so, he must have made Balfour his accomplice, which would account for Balfour's appointment in the spring to the governorship of Edinburgh Castle, a trust characteristically betrayed, surrendering the castle without a blow to Mary and Bothwell's enemies.

Nothing too sinister need be read into the unmarked condition of the bodies of Darnley and his valet. The suggestion that they were murdered after escaping to the garden seems absurd; they would hardly have carried a quilt and a kitchen chair with them. It is more likely, as Eric Linklater argued, that they were thrown there by the blast. He pointed out that experience of the effects of bombing in the Second World War had demonstrated the queer tricks that an explosion could play. 'That, surely, is what happened at Kirk o' Field. The cellar loaded with gunpowder blew up like a land mine, and blew through the shattered roof of the house not only two dead bodies but the quilt, dressing gown and that unnecessary chair. The bodies were, on the surface, unmarked, and there was no pathologist to conduct a post-mortem and establish the cause of death . . .' This is at least a plausible explanation.

Whatever the truth of the case, Darnley's murder affords us an instructive view of the Edinburgh of the time. One cannot fail to remark the intimacy of the place: everything happened within a small area and was open to the intense scrutiny of an interested and sometimes violent public. The faults of the Stewart monarchs could never be divorced from the influence of public opinion. They lived among their people, and they maintained their privileges with great difficulty. Almost forty years later, Mary's son, James VI, was involved in a long struggle with another Bothwell, Francis Stewart Hepburn, who was the nephew of both Mary's third husband and her half-brother Moray. This wild man, suspected of witchcraft, distressed him for years, and even terrorised him. On one occasion he abducted a witness from the Tolbooth in Edinburgh, while the king was in the next room. Two years later, on 14 July 1593, James was awakened by a commotion and discovered that his cousin was in possession of Holyrood. He fled towards the queen's bedchamber, shouting, 'Treason', but found the door bolted. Other nobles then broke into the palace and persuaded the king to open negotiations with Bothwell, who had earlier been declared an outlaw. Meanwhile a crowd of armed citizens had gathered round the palace. James stuck his head out of the window and told them to go home, assuring them in blunt and unkingly terms that the danger was past and he was again master of the situation. In such an atmosphere, the pretensions of royalty were inevitably diluted.

Skirmishes and riots, not always political in origin, were frequent in the city streets. In 1567, for instance, a burgess by the name of Birrel noted in his diary: 'The 24 of November, at two afternoon, the Laird of Airth and the Laird of Weems met on the High Gate of Edinburgh, and they and their followers fought a very bloody skirmish, where there were many hurt on both sides with shot of pistol.' Such incidents were common in a society where men regularly went armed and were quick to pursue hereditary quarrels and ancient feuds. The difficulties the Crown experienced in keeping order were intensified by the rivalry not only of great families but also of petty lairds.

Yet it was politics which most disturbed the everyday life of the growing city. After the evaporation of her army at Carberry Hill, and Bothwell's flight, Mary was brought back to Edinburgh and exposed to the insults of the mob. Four days later she was imprisoned in the island castle of Loch Leven, where she was compelled to abdicate, while in Edinburgh the General Assembly of the Kirk hurried on a more perfect reformation, and the zealously Protestant Earl of Glencairn took it upon himself to destroy the furnishings of Mary's private chapel at Holyrood. In May 1568 the queen, whose abdication had been extorted by threats to her life, and whose infant son had already been crowned James VI, escaped from her prison, and, finding support from the great Hamilton family in the West, raised another army. This was scattered at Langside just south of

Glasgow, and Mary fled to England to throw herself on the mercy of her cousin Elizabeth, in the hope that Elizabeth would restore her to the throne. Very soon Scotland was in the grip of a sporadic civil war, centring on the control of Edinburgh. The war between the revolutionaries (the King's Men) and the Queen's Men who were loyal to Mary and hoped for her restoration lasted for six years. Edinburgh mirrored the split in the country. There were two town councils and two kirk sessions – the King's Men from the burgh setting up a civic government-in-exile down at the port of Leith. Both sides held Parliaments in the city. In May 1571 they were even held at the same time – the Queen's Men in the Tolbooth and the King's Men in the Canongate, outside the burgh walls, where they were bombarded from the castle which was held by Mary's supporters, and quickly ended their session. This 'creeping parliament' lasted less than half an hour, but found time to declare the lands of leading Queen's Men forfeit. The Marians replied with a rival list, and the houses of thirty supporters of the king who had fled from the city were demolished.

It was a war of propaganda also, for opinion was volatile and therefore worth persuading. Thomas Bassenden printed fifteen Marian tracts at his press in Edinburgh; Robert Lepreuik, the official printer to the General Assembly, fled from Edinburgh to St Andrews to carry on his work.

A truce was arranged in May 1572, but soon broken by the civic government-in-exile who marched into Edinburgh and resumed control. The defeated party were compelled to appear before the kirk session, bare-headed and in sackcloth, to confess their sins; they were also fined for good measure.

Meanwhile the Queen's Men, commanded by Mary's former secretary, Maitland of Lethington, and Kirkcaldy of Grange (loyal to the queen despite being a Protestant), still held the castle. It was then besieged by the new regent, the sour and sinister Earl of Morton, but he had to call for English assistance to take it. The arrival of English gunners led to a bombardment lasting four days. The garrison surrendered on the promise of safe conduct, a promise that Morton characteristically broke. Maitland died in obscure circumstances and Kirkcaldy of Grange was executed, as were two Edinburgh goldsmiths who had been minting coin in the castle. One of them, James Mossman, was the owner of the building in the High Street which is now called John Knox's House. The victory was celebrated at St Giles; Knox's successor as minister gave thanks to Queen Elizabeth for the deliverance of city and country from the hand of the ungodly.

The years from 1573 to the Union of the Crowns in 1603 saw the gradual re-establishment of royal authority. Morton, as regent, had a part in this, being ruthless in the extraction of money to boost the precarious royal finances. It was a time of uncertainty and tension, for the old quarrels were not yet resolved. Morton himself would fall victim to them, or at least to his own past: in 1580 he was accused in the Privy Council of complicity in the murder of Darnley, a convenient charge which could neither be proved nor disproved. He was condemned to death and executed. He suffered by means of a primitive guillotine called the 'Maiden' which he had himself introduced into Scotland.

Religious strife continued also, though it was now as fierce between extreme Calvinists and Moderates as it had formerly been between Catholics and Reformers, not that fears of a Catholic revival were yet extinct. A body of religious police, known as 'seizers', had been formed to maintain discipline and morality: in 1570 two men, one a blacksmith, had been burned on the Castle Hill 'for committing the horrible sin of sodomy'. The anonymous author of the *Diurnal of Occurrents* remarked that 'in no time heretofore was it heard that any persons in this country were found guilty of this crime', though many asserted of course that it had been a common monastic practice. The next victims were a brother and sister named Bonar, accused of having 'carnal copulation together'. The 'seizers' were objects of fear and resentment. There was therefore some rejoicing when one of them, Robert Drummond, described as a 'great seeker and apprehender of all priests and Papists', was found in the bed of another man's wife. The pair were consigned to the stocks, where Drummond 'being in a great fury' (and no wonder) 'took his own knife, and struck himself three or four times foranent the heart, with which he departed. This done, the magistrates caused hurl

him in a cart through the town, and the bloody knife borne
behind in his hand . . .' But the 'seizers' who were to survive into
the eighteenth century were evidence of a moral rigour that was
to make Edinburgh life frequently uncomfortable, and which also
provoked hypocrisy and the assumption of a superior virtue not
always in accordance with reality.

 Towards the end of the century the English traveller Fynes
Morrison left a vivid description of the city:

> This City is high seated, in a fruitful soil, and wholesome
> air, and it is adorned with many noblemen's towers lying
> about it, and abounds with many springs of sweet waters.
> At the end towards the east is the king's palace joining to
> the monastery of the Holy Cross, which King David the
> first built, over which, in a park of hares, conies and deer,

View of Edinburgh in the late
16th century:
Braun & Hoggenbourg print

a high mountain hangs, called the chair of Arthur (of Arthur, the prince of Britons, whose monuments, famous among all ballad-makers, are for the most part to be found on these borders of England and Scotland). From the King's palace at the east the city rises higher and higher to the west, and consists especially of one broad and very fair street (which is the greatest part and sole ornament thereof), the rest of the side streets and alleys being of poor building and inhabited with very poor people, and this length from the east to the west is about a mile, whereas the breadth of the city from the north to the south is narrow, and cannot be half a mile. At the furthest end towards the west is a very strong castle which the Scots hold expugnable, and from the castle towards the west is a most steep rock pointed on the highest top, out of which this castle is cut: but on the north and south sides without the walls, lie plain and fruitful fields of corn. In the midst of the foresaid fair street, the Cathedral church is built, which is large and lightsome, but little stately for the building, and nothing at all for beauty and ornament.

This was a flattering, yet sufficiently accurate, description of the city James VI knew, even though the English visitor was mistaken in his assumption that St Giles was a cathedral, a status it was not granted till 1633. It was the parish kirk of Edinburgh, which was still only one parish, though the church was so divided as to serve three distinct congregations.

In 1603 James VI would inherit the English throne, and become James I of England. From his residence in the south he would boast that he ruled Scotland more easily with the pen than his ancestors had done with the sword, but in 1596 he had been given a sharp taste of the temper of 'the poor people' of his native city, whom Morrison so easily dismissed. It was a time of renewed religious agitation, perhaps inspired by fears that the king favoured the Catholic lords of the north-east. At any rate, though much remains mysterious, there was a deal of fiery preaching, one minister, David Black of St Andrews, launching an attack on James's wife, Anne of Denmark, and even on Elizabeth of England, whose government was then engaged in the suppression of the extreme Puritans south of the border. A rioting mob surrounded the king and the Lords of Session who

James VI and I
(anon.)

were then meeting in the Tolbooth. James temporised, but as soon as possible removed himself from the city to his palace at Linlithgow, and commanded the Court of Session to be transferred to Perth. He issued a proclamation condemning 'the late treasonable uproar' and the seditious sermons which had referred to himself 'in a most irreverent manner with speeches illbefitting any subject'. The implication was plain: if Edinburgh persisted in such tumultuous behaviour it would lose its status as the seat of government and law. Some of his courtiers even advised him to raze the city to the ground. The Town Council got the message, the Lord Provost denying any foreknowledge 'of that unworthy and unhappy tumult that suddenly fell out'. He even appealed to Elizabeth to intercede on Edinburgh's behalf. The king, having made his point, relented: the 'irreverent preachers' were banished, the minister's house in the kirkyard of St Giles was made over to the king, and he was granted £20,000 for the refurbishment of Holyrood. James had done rather well out of the riot, and the City Fathers learned which side their bread was buttered on.

James VI, nervous, sometimes irresolute, often devious, was nevertheless firm in his purpose, which was to inherit the throne of England. In pursuit of this ambition he had acquiesced in the execution of his mother, contenting himself with delivering a feeble protest to Elizabeth. Eventually, though she refused to name an heir, the way opened before him. There was no credible alternative, and Elizabeth's minister Robert Cecil became James's confidant and advocate. Early in the morning of Thursday 25 March 1603, the old queen at last died.

On the evening of the 26th, James and his queen had retired to bed in Holyrood when a banging was heard at the outer gate. It was opened to admit an Englishman, Sir Robert Carey. He had left Whitehall between nine and ten on the Thursday morning, and ridden hard, with several changes of horse, to Edinburgh. He arrived there, his head bloody from a fall and a kick from his horse, and insisted on being presented immediately to the king. He threw himself on his knees before James, who was in a dressing gown: 'Queen Elizabeth is dead, and Your Majesty is

King of England.'

Even so, James prudently waited till he received formal notice from the Privy Council in London, and it was not till 5 April that he left Holyrood, with a great train of attendants, both Scots and English.

Two days previously, he had said farewell to his Scottish subjects in a sermon delivered at St Giles. 'There is no more difference,' he told them, 'betwixt London and Edinburgh, yea, not so much, as betwixt Inverness or Aberdeen, for all our marches are dry and there be ferries betwixt them . . . Ye must not doubt but, as I have a body as able as any king in Europe, whereby I am able to travel, so I sall visit you every three year at the least, or ofter as I sall have occasion.'

But it was to be fourteen years before the king was back in his native city again.

3

The Seventeenth Century

It might be thought that the departure of the king and court would have adversely affected the city. No doubt something was lost, but in fact the first decades of the seventeenth century were fruitful. A small portion of the nobility had, it is true, accompanied the king south, and other nobles fell into the habit of presenting themselves at Whitehall from time to time; but for the most part they maintained residences in Edinburgh, where they still attended the meetings of the Scottish Parliament. Nor did either James or his son Charles I neglect their northern capital. James had inaugurated the Townis College in 1582. On his visit in 1617 he took part in a debate with its professors, and congratulated them on the quality of their Latin pronunciation, which, he said, reminded him of his tutor, the erudite though crabbit Buchanan. He called the building of the college 'a work so universally beneficial to our subjects and of such ornament and reputation for our city in particular', and granted it the name of 'King James' College'. The title has not adhered: in time the Townis College became the University of Edinburgh.

Five years later the great goldsmith and merchant George Heriot, 'Jingling Geordie' (vividly portrayed by Scott in *The Fortunes of Nigel*), bequeathed a great part of his fortune for 'the founding and erecting of a hospital . . . to be employed for the maintenance, relief, bringing up and education of so many poor fatherless boys, freemen's sons of the town of Edinburgh'. His example would be followed by other Edinburgh merchants. The building, by William Aytoun, is a masterpiece of the Northern Renaissance, perhaps the finest school building in Scotland.

*The Arms of King James'
College, 1617*
(University of Edinburgh)

Statue of George Heriot
by Robert Mylne
in the courtyard of Heriot's
School (Hospital)

At the same time the east wing of the castle was rebuilt, the architect being probably the king's master mason Sir James Murray, also responsible for reconstruction of the south wing and gallery of Holyrood in preparation for Charles I's coronation in 1633. Of more significance was Murray's Parliament House, begun in 1632 on the site of the houses which had originally belonged to the prebendaries of St Giles and had been granted to the king in 1597. The building of Parliament House gave the city its first square, between it and St Giles, far more animated than it is today, since it was lined with the shops of goldsmiths, watchmakers and bookbinders. The book trade was profitable: 'One Edinburgh printer who specialised in schoolbooks had in

George Heriot's School (Hospital) by Paul Sandby, c. 1750

*James III with St Andrew and
Prince James (?)*
from the Trinity Altarpiece
by Hugo van der Goes

The Murder of Rizzio by Sir William Allan

The Signing of the National Covenant by Sir William Allan

Gladstone's Land – the Painted Chamber

Montrose led to Execution
by James Drummond

The Several Journals of the
Court of Directors of the
Company of Scotland trading
to Africa and the Indies:
title page

The Downsitting of Parliament: the Scottish parliament in session in the late 17th century, from the French *Atlas Historique*, published in 1721

The Porteous Mob at the Tolbooth, 1736 (anon.)

Horsefair on Bruntsfield Links by Paul Sandby, 1750

Prince Charles Edward Stuart at Holyrood, 1745 by William Hole

1622 over 1500 bound Latin books and over 39,000 unbound "for skoles", mostly grammars or Virgils; he had in addition 2300 bound and 42,000 unbound small books in English, which must mostly have been for use in the vernacular schools."*

It was a time of mercantile expansion. The population of Edinburgh seems to have doubled between 1580 and 1630, and there was a corresponding economic development. This was reflected in the number of merchants' houses rising in the Lawnmarket. One of these, Gladstone's Land, survives today. It was built about 1600, six storeys high and fronted with an arcade at street level, and acquired by the merchant Thomas Gledstanes in 1617. He sold off most of the tenement and lived on the top floor himself, relatively free from the stench of the street middens.

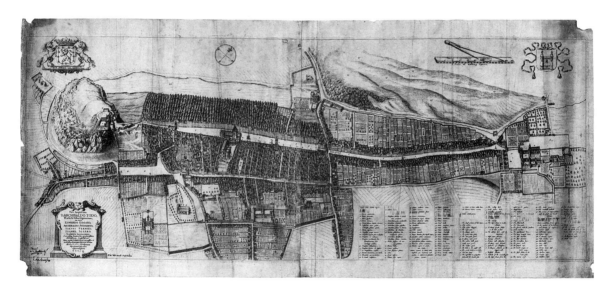

Bird's-eye view of Edinburgh, 1647
by James Gordon of Rothiemay

The establishment of civic peace and the temporary lulling of sectarian conflict encouraged concentration on business. There were at least three hundred Edinburgh merchants with interests in international trade. Hides, leather, salt, coal, herrings, rope and lead were all exported from Leith. Factors were maintained in the principal ports of northern Europe. Sir William Dick of Braid, Lord Provost of Edinburgh in 1638, had been able to advance £6,000 to James VI twenty years earlier. He had interests

* Lynch.

Gladstone's Land

in herring-processing, salt-pans, coal mines and granaries; he farmed the customs, extended the trade of the Firth of Forth, and financed Montrose's campaign during the Bishops' Wars. He was knighted by Charles I and made a baronet of Nova Scotia. In 1650 he lent £20,000 to Charles II (who had been proclaimed King of Scots by the Scottish Parliament within a few days of his father's execution on 30 January 1649). The debt was never repaid and the fine imposed by Cromwell reduced him to destitution. He died in a debtors' prison, according to some accounts, but his earlier splendour was more remarkable than his final misfortunes.

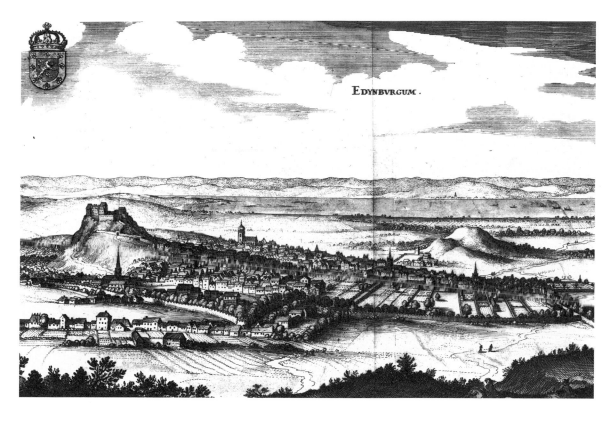

EDYNBVRGVM.

View of Edinburgh, mid 17th century from the south. The port of Leith is shown in the distance

The merchants were rivalled, even outstripped, by the lawyers. James V's establishment of the Court of Session in Edinburgh had concentrated the nation's legal activity in the capital. Within thirty years the combined wealth of thirty-one lawyers was greater than that of a quarter of Edinburgh's 350 merchants. In 1636 a Highland chief, McLeod of Dunvegan, spent £3,600 in legal fees. The great families of the law – Scotland's *noblesse de la robe* – Hopes, Dundases, Clerks and Dalrymples – all came to the fore in the seventeenth century. They mostly played their cards cannily: Sir Thomas Hope of Craighall, Lord Advocate in 1626, moved smoothly from being the king's servant to a position in the covenanting administration. It may well be that the departure of the court eased the advancement of the lawyers. Certainly the legal profession in England never achieved the dominance of its Scottish counterpart, or crystallised into an almost distinct caste as was the case in Edinburgh.

The promise of the early seventeenth century was interrupted by the events of 1637–50, which may indeed be described as the Second Scottish Revolution (the first being of course the Reformation). This revolution was provoked by the folly of Charles I and his advisers, determined to secure religious uniformity throughout the two kingdoms.

The occasion of the revolution was the introduction of a new Prayer Book. It provoked a riot in St Giles and in the other churches of the city. The demonstration was almost certainly planned: the intention to use the new liturgy had been announced from the pulpits the previous Sunday. The Dean of St Giles, at whose head a stool had been thrown, was compelled to take refuge in the steeple tower of the cathedral; the bishop fled to Holyrood in a borrowed coach, pelted with stones throughout the journey. Discontent continued to rumble. In a few months the King's Council thought it wise to remove to Linlithgow and the city was abandoned to the rebels.

The cause of the revolution went deeper. It was essentially the result of a gradual breakdown of communication between the king and the different estates of the realm, all of whom had in one way or another been alienated by a government which seemed unwilling to listen to reason, and determined to have its own way. A crucial element in fomenting discontent was the Act of Revocation which Charles had pronounced in 1625. Originally this seemed an attempt to resume lands alienated by the Crown over the past century. Then it emerged that it applied to Church lands also. Since there was scarcely a landowning family or burgh which had not benefited from the secularisation of Church property at the time of the Reformation, this seemed to threaten

The Book of Common Prayer:
'. . . for the use of the
Church of Scotland'.
Title page, 1637

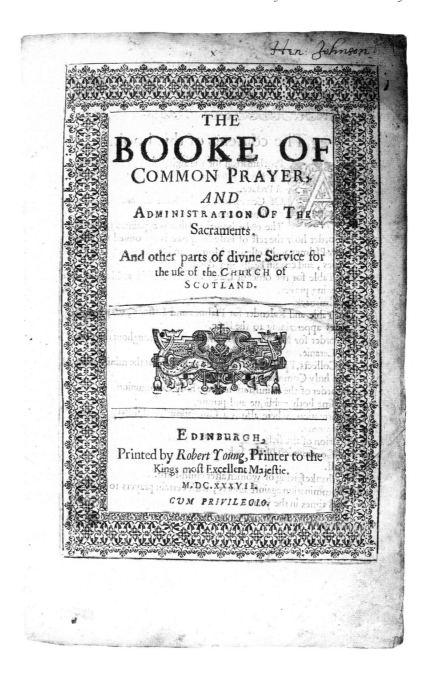

the very basis of property rights. If the king could do this, whose
estates were safe?

Second, as in England, Charles, desperate for money as the
expenses of government increased and the returns from traditional sources of revenue, especially Crown lands which were

often let on long leases, diminished, had imposed new, heavier and in some cases dubiously legal taxes on his subjects. Edinburgh found itself paying more in tax in the first two years of his reign than it had paid in the last twenty of King James's.

There was therefore festering discontent even before Charles attempted his liturgical reforms. The language of revolution would be religious, but the revolution itself arose from the threat to the interests of the propertied classes. The ministers of the kirk, by no means all friendly to the authority claimed by the nobility, were nevertheless the natural and popular spokesmen of the revolution in its early phases.

In November 1637, after the King's Council had left the city, an important step was taken. With the approval of the Lord Advocate, Sir Thomas Hope, commissioners were appointed who formed themselves into four committees – nobles, lairds, burgesses and ministers – henceforth known as 'the Tables'. 'It was,' as John Buchan wrote, 'in substance a provisional government, and behind it was all Scotland, except the remoter Highlands and Aberdeen.'

Charles, the distinguishing mark of whose character was obstinacy, announced in February 1638 that he took full responsibility for the new liturgy; he ordered the dissidents to disperse on pain of treason and not to reassemble without the council's consent. It was a proclamation which he had no means of enforcing, and the riposte, long-prepared, was immediate. A National Covenant was drawn up, drafted by Alexander Henderson, minister of Leuchars, and Johnston of Warriston, a zealot in a lawyer's gown. It asserted the right to both spiritual and civil liberty, and on the last day of February 1638 it was read from the pulpit of Greyfriars Church. Its legality was guaranteed by the Lord Advocate, and nobles, lairds, burgesses and ministers subscribed their names over the next two days among the tombstones in the wintry kirkyard. It was one of the most solemn and momentous days in Edinburgh's history.

The country was preparing for war. Johnston of Warriston records in his diary a sermon preached in Edinburgh on 1 April when the minister, Mr Rollock, first read the Covenant, and then asked the nobles present, who included the young Montrose, to hold up their hands and swear by the name of the living God: 'At the which instant of rising up, and then of holding up their hands, there arose sic a yelloch, sic abundance of tears, sic a heavenly harmony of sighs and sobs, universally through all the corners of the church, as the like was never seen nor heard of.' It would have required a wiser statesman than Charles I to restore calm and amity.

Edinburgh was zealous for the Covenant, even though the castle was still held for the king, and the king's navy was seen in the Firth of Forth. But the Provost of Edinburgh felt sufficiently secure in the faith to defy the king's command that he should proclaim the Covenanting Earl of Argyll an outlaw at the Mercat Cross. Instead he informed Charles that 'in such troublesome times . . . he durst scarcely hazard to make any such proclamation against the person of such a prime nobleman'. Besides which, he told the king, he was doubtful if the royal request was agreeable to the Law of Scotland. Instead he set himself to provision the Covenanting army; all the silver in the city was melted down for coins to pay the soldiers, though the council was careful to secure promise of repayment 'in the current money according to weight'. Meanwhile the Royalists in the castle were starved into surrender, though not before it was calculated that almost two hundred citizens had been killed by fire from the castle.

Already, however, the General Assembly had met in Edinburgh, and then a historic Parliament which had abolished episcopacy and severely restricted the royal prerogative. Charles himself visited Edinburgh after the short Bishops' War in an attempt to restore his position. He promoted enemies in the nobility, but to no avail, and it was during this visit, while playing golf on the links at Leith, that he received news of the Irish Rebellion which was to be the trigger for the Civil War that convulsed the three kingdoms.

Edinburgh played little part in the first Civil War, for Scotland was quiet till 1644 under the rule of the Covenant, and Montrose's campaign in the king's interest took place north of the Highland Line. But after his victory at Kilsyth in August 1645, there was fear in the capital. The Town Council organised itself for defence. The town wall was repaired, and new gates were built, one at the bottom of Leith Wynd and the other at the Pleasance. The Trained Bands were ordered to stand guard all night, and citizens were forbidden to leave the city without the permission of the magistrates, whom they were also obliged to furnish with 'the name and quality of their several lodgers, under pain of £1000 Scots and loss of their freedom forever'. But Montrose contented himself with demanding the release of Royalist prisoners who included his uncle, Napier of Merchiston, the deviser of logarithms, and did not approach the city, which was in any case ravaged by an outbreak of the plague, so severe that it was said that 'there were scarcely 50 men left capable of assisting the defence of the town in case of an attack'.

James Graham, 1st Marquess of Montrose
by William Dobson

The threat was not to be renewed, for Montrose's brilliant campaign ended in his surprise defeat by General David Leslie at Philiphaugh in the Borders, and the king soon surrendered himself to the Covenanting army, whose chiefs, after months of negotiations, sold him to the English Parliament. Three years of confused politics followed, as the different parties sought a way out of the uncertainties in which a decade of revolutionary politics and war had cast them. The split in the Covenanters led to the Engagement by which the more moderate of the king's enemies undertook to restore him to such power as was agreeable to them, but the Engagers' army was defeated by Cromwell at Preston, and its leader, the Duke of Hamilton, executed. An old woman remarked, 'Folks said it wasna a very gude head, but it was a sair loss to him, puir gentleman.' For its support of the Engagement the Edinburgh Town Council was purged, the godly Covenanters being more ruthless in the exercise of power than any Stewart king had dared to be.

The king was put on trial by the Rump of the English Parliament, and beheaded at Whitehall on 30 January 1649. This outraged all but the most extreme Covenanters, and his son was almost immediately proclaimed king by the Scots Parliament. The young Charles was not yet ready to be a Covenanted king. He spun out negotiations, even while commissioning Montrose to raise a Royalist army. When Montrose failed and was betrayed to his enemies by Neil Macleod of Assynt, to whom he had looked for help, Charles had already come to an agreement with the Covenant. He seems to have assumed – the evidence is conflicting – that he had made arrangements to secure the safety of his captain-general. If so, he deceived himself. Montrose was to be hustled out of the way before the king could reach Scotland.

He was brought to Edinburgh for execution. There was to be no trial, for he had already been sentenced to death in 1644 when he first took arms against the Covenant which, back in Greyfriars churchyard, he had been one of the first to sign.

He arrived at Leith about four o'clock on the afternoon of Saturday 20 May, and was conveyed to the Watergate at the bottom of the Canongate, where the hangman's cart awaited him. His hands were tied behind his back, and it was piously hoped that the crowd would express their hatred by throwing dung and stones at him.

There are many accounts of his entry to Edinburgh, but the best is John Buchan's:

> Slowly, in the bright evening, the procession moved up the Via Dolorosa of Scottish history. The street was lined by a great crowd – the dregs of the Edinburgh slums, the retainers of the Covenanting lords, ministers from far and near – all the elements most bitterly hostile to the prisoner. But to the amazement of the organizers of the spectacle there was no sign of popular wrath. Rather there was silence, a tense air of sympathy and pity and startled admiration . . . In the strained quiet, broken only by excited sobs, there was one jarring note. Lady Jean Gordon, Lord Haddington's widow, Argyll's niece and Huntly's daughter, is said to have laughed shrilly and shouted a word of insult from the balcony where she sat. A voice cried out of the crowd that the right place for her was in the hangman's cart to expiate her sins.
>
> In the lodgings along the Canongate the Covenant chiefs were assembled to witness the degradation of their enemy. In the balcony of Lord Moray's house Lord Lorne sat with his young bride, Lady Mary Stewart, the same man who, thirty-five years later, was himself to go to a not inglorious scaffold. Inside the house, with the shutters half-closed, stood Argyll, with Loudoun and Warriston. Montrose, as he passed, caught a glimpse of the anxious unhappy face which he knew so well, and for the first time for long the two men looked into each other's eyes . . . The shutters were closed and the faces disappeared. There was an English soldier in the crowd who observed the incident and cried, 'It was no wonder they started aside at his look, for they durst not look him in the face these seven years bygone.'

The next day being the Sabbath, there were fierce sermons throughout the city, directed at Montrose and reproaching the mob for their forbearance or decency. He had been lodged in the Tolbooth, where he was visited by a squad of ministers and by the Provost of Edinburgh, Sir James Stewart of Coltness who, to his credit, had protested against the barbarity of the sentence – 'so much butchery and dismembering'. On the Monday he was taken before the Parliament to hear his sentence. It was read by

Warriston, and Montrose lifted his head as he spoke and looked him in the eye.

That night in his prison under the eye of the town guard, whose captain was a Major Weir (of whom more later), he wrote his last poem:

> Let them bestow on every airth a limb,
> Then open all my veins, that I may swim
> To thee, my Maker, in that crimson lake;
> Then place my parboiled head upon a stake,
> Scatter my ashes, strew them in the air. –
> Lord, since thou knowest where all these atoms are,
> I'm hopeful Thou'lt recover all my dust,
> And confident Thou'lt raise me with the just.

He was hanged about half-past two the following afternoon at the Mercat Cross. One witness, the notary public John Nicoll, said he resembled a bridegroom rather than a criminal. The crowd maintained a decent silence – Buchan calls it 'reverent' – till the moment of death, when a great sob sounded, and tears were observed even on the hangman's face.

The Gaelic poet Ian Lom Macdonald wrote:

> I'll not go to Dunedin
> Since the Graham's blood was shed
> The manly mighty lion
> Tortured on the gallows.
>
> That was the true gentleman,
> Who came of line not humble,
> Good was the flushing of his cheek
> When drawing up to combat.

But the extreme Covenanters, who were in the ascendancy in the city, thought differently; the execution was the deliverance of the godly, and powerful testimony to the favour of the Almighty.

Charles soon arrived in Scotland, but was not yet crowned king, having instead to endure many hours of sermons while the preachers dilated on his wickedness and that of his late father. Meanwhile the Covenanting army was purged of all who were not staunch in the narrowest expression of the faith, or who had compromised themselves by any previous Royalist association. It was a strange way to secure the new king's throne, and unfortunately the purge deprived General David Leslie of many of his most experienced officers. Instead, a committee of ministers and godly elders constituted themselves his General Staff, and when Cromwell advanced north, they compelled Leslie to abandon the advantage he had secured over the English army and descend into the plain by Dunbar to smite the Amalekite. Unfortunately, the godly were themselves smitten, despite their superiority in number, and the humiliation at Dunbar was complete. Leslie withdrew into the city (which he shortly abandoned, leaving only a garrison to hold the castle), the Town Council and Kirk Session fled across the Forth, some as far as Dundee, the ministers who remained in the city also withdrew into the castle, and their churches were given over to Cromwell's army, who used them as ammunition stores. When the castle was surrendered to Cromwell without a fight, which was both a surprise and a relief to him, since he admitted that 'little or nothing' else could have been attempted if he had been compelled to lay siege to it, the Godly Revolution, which had begun in 1637, was effectively at an end.

It had cost Scotland and Edinburgh dear. The unity of the Church had been broken, and would indeed never be thoroughly repaired. Scotland was occupied by an English army. Plague and war had destroyed trade; perhaps 20 per cent of town dwellers had died of plague, and the economic situation was so bad that Edinburgh rents were reduced by a third in 1651. Even so bankruptcies were numerous, Sir William Dick being only the most conspicuous among them.

Scotland was forcibly incorporated into a Union, proclaimed at the Mercat Cross in April 1652. Three days later the Royal Arms were hauled down from the cross and ceremonially hanged from the public gallows. The country was subjected to unprecedentedly heavy taxation. Charles I's unpopular taxes had cost Scotland about £17,000 a year. The Cromwellian government fixed a monthly assessment of £10,000, principally to pay for the army of occupation. Even the liberty of conscience for which some believed they had fought was denied them. In 1653

Cromwell's troopers interrupted the proceedings of the General Assembly, and ejected its members.

Yet, as Michael Lynch has written, 'Much of Scottish history is fuelled by myths; the most important for many in the second half of the seventeenth century was the cherished myth of the Covenanters that the Reformed Church had come in 1648 to "the top of her perfection and glory" and that in 1650 "her sun went down at noon".'

4

Restoration to Union

In that mythic version of Scottish history the reigns of Charles II and James VII were bitterly recorded. It was 'the Killing Time' when the Saints were hunted down on the western moors by Claverhouse and other malignants. The picture is etched in the imagination. Even Stevenson, caught at that point of conflict, characteristic of the Scottish mind, where Tory and Covenanting sympathies join together, remembered from Samoa 'where about the graves of the martyrs the whaups are crying'.

> Grey recumbent tombs of the dead in desert places,
> Standing-stones on the vacant wine-red moor,
> Hills of sheep and the howes of the silent vanished races,
> And winds austere and pure.

Few Scots, few Lowlanders anyway, can fail to respond to the myth of the Covenanters as 'a suffering remnant of the House of Israel'. It is an enduring and potent image we carry with us: the little Conventicle singing psalms and worshipping the Lord in the western moorlands while sentries scan the tops for the approach of the godless dragoons.

There is some truth in it, as in all myths. And that truth is supported by other memories: of the Kirkyard of Greyfriars, ironically the scene of triumph forty years earlier when the nation came together to subscribe to the Covenant; now in 1679, after the Battle of Bothwell Brig, thronged with more than a thousand captured Saints, living in barbarous conditions without shelter from July to November, some awaiting execution in the Grassmarket below, others transportation to slavery in Barbados, Jamaica or the Carolinas.

Condemned Covenanters on their way to Execution (anon.)

Yet powerful as the image is, it is deceptive for two reasons. First, the extreme Covenanters who were the victims of the restored monarchy were but a tiny remnant, for most Scots accepted the Church Settlement of 1661–2, even if many grumbled at it. Moreover the Dissidents were extremists, committed to overthrowing the monarchy and re-establishing the severe and far more intolerant theocracy of 1648. The heroes of the movement were the men who assassinated Archbishop Sharp, dragging him from his coach on Magus Muir in Fife to kill him before the eyes of his daughter.

Second, the myth hides from us the reality that the reigns of the Stewart brothers were a time of renewed prosperity after the turmoil and economic depression brought about by the wars; this was especially so in Edinburgh. The nobility gradually recovered from the destitution with which war and the exactions of the Republican government had threatened them, and to which some had actually been reduced: the Earl of Traquair, Lord Treasurer in Charles I's Privy Council, was found begging in the High Street shortly before his death in 1659, without the means 'even to paye for cobling his bootes'. Others were deep in debt. This was caused partly by a shortage of liquidity, for many debtors were creditors of others, desperately seeking what was owed them to pay what they owed themselves. When the king came into his own again, government service, with the opportunities for the exercise of patronage and the receiving of bribes which it offered, was a way out for some; more efficient exploitation of their estates for others.

The results may be seen in the number of country houses built or enlarged in this period: the Duke of Lauderdale's Thirlstane Castle, Queensberry's Drumlanrig (though the duke is said to have spent only one night there), Hamilton's Hamilton Palace. More evidence of renewed confidence and resources was provided by the building of new noble mansions or the refurbishment of existing ones in the still fashionable Canongate. Queensberry House, a large, gloomy building enclosed in a court on the south side of the street, is one example, occupied much of the time by the duchess alone, an unfortunate woman, given to drink and kept short of supplies. These mansions resembled the

Moray House and Canongate Tolbooth
by John le Conte, 1886

Canongate Tolbooth Moray House looking up to Tron Church. John le Conte 1886
Edinburgh. No. 60

town houses, or palaces, of the French nobility in Paris, before Louis XIV concentrated his court at Versailles. Moray House, which still stands, had extensive south-facing gardens to the rear, said to be 'of such elegance, and cultivated with so much care, as to vie with those of warmer countries, and perhaps even of England itself'. They showed how 'the art and industry of man may avail in supplying the defects of nature. Scarcely any one would believe it is possible to give so much beauty to a garden in this frigid clime.' These gardens have long ago disappeared, lost as Lyonnesse beneath the modern College of Education.

It was in Charles II's reign also that Holyrood assumed the appearance it still bears. Lauderdale, in effect the Viceroy of Scotland, commissioned Sir William Bruce, the architect also of his own Thirlstane, to repair the damage inflicted by Cromwell's troopers and complete the building planned by James V. Ironically, the finished palace was not even to be visited by a reigning monarch till George IV made his famous state visit to Scotland in 1822. Even then, he did not occupy the palace,

The Palace of Holyroodhouse: engraving after P. Fourdrinier, 1751

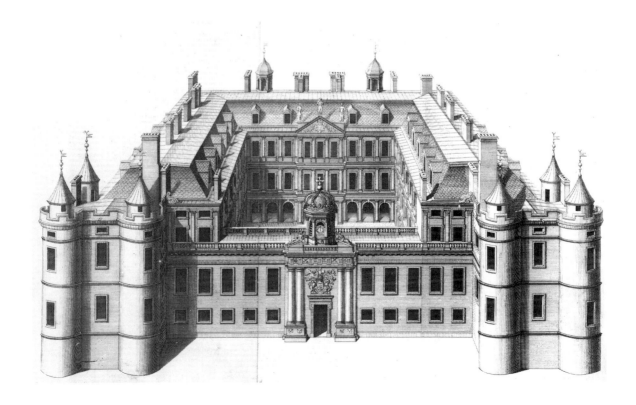

preferring to be the Duke of Buccleuch's guest at Dalkeith. However, James VII, as Duke of York, lived in Holyrood in 1679, when he succeeded Lauderdale as Viceroy. Fifty years later, according to Robert Chambers, 'old people used to talk with delight of the magnificency and brilliancy of the Court which James assembled, and of the general tone of happiness and satisfaction which pervaded the town on this occasion'. The happiness and satisfaction were somewhat diminished by James's decision to use the abbey as a Catholic chapel, even though one consequence of this was the building of the splendid Canongate Kirk for the displaced congregation of the abbey.

Whatever the nobility thought of James's court – and they were pleased by his revival of the Order of the Knights of the Thistle whose stalls were in the Abbey Chapel – the mob who thronged the wynds and closes off the High Street and Canongate took a different view of this papistry. When revolution broke out in 1688, and the Roman Catholic Earl of Perth, the chancellor, made a hurried departure, 'the mob made it a signal for an attack on Holyrood Chapel. A body of a hundred men defended it with firearms, which they freely used against their assailants, killing twelve of them and wounding many more. But this only increased the fury of the mob; the armed defenders were at length overpowered, and the chapel delivered up to their will. The magnificent carved stalls, which had just been completed, and all the costly fittings of the chapel were reduced to an unsightly heap of ruins.'*

Despite the fate of his chapel (which with the other abbey ruins was to become a sanctuary for debtors), James's brief residence in the city left some more permanent memorials. The Merchant Company, famous among other things for its educational foundations, dates from 1681, and a piazza was built for the merchants in Parliament Square. James also revived the royal bodyguard, the Royal Company of Archers, who still perform ceremonial duties when the queen visits her northern capital. James became patron of the Royal College of Physicians (1681) and extended his support to the Physic Garden in the grounds of

* Sir Daniel Wilson, *Memorials of Edinburgh in the Olden Time.*

Trinity Hospital, where Waverley Station is now; this was the creation of Sir Robert Sibbald, Geographer-Royal and King's Physician, and Dr Andrew Balfour. Its purpose was practical: to discover what medicinal herbs could be grown in Scotland, but it was to be the forerunner of the Botanic Gardens in Inverleith. Sibbald serves as an illustration of the slowly changing temper of society. Originally intended for the Church, he declared that 'I saw none could enter to the ministrie without indulging in factions. I preferred a quiet life, wherein I might not be ingadged in factions of Church or State. I fixed upon the studie of medicine wherein I thought I might be of no faction and might be useful to my generation.'

Sir George Mackenzie, the Lord Advocate, could not have claimed any comparable disinclination to engage in factional or party dispute. His persecution of the Covenanters earned him the sobriquet 'the Bluidy Mackenzie'. Nevertheless, Sir George's cultural interests were wide; his *Institutions of the Law of Scotland* (1684) gave a coherent philosophical structure to the criminal law.

Sir George Mackenzie
after Sir Godfrey Kneller

He founded the Advocates' Library, from which the National Library of Scotland would eventually be born, and he wrote a prose romance, *Aretina*, which is said to be the first Scottish novel. He was also an enthusiast for the Scots tongue, proclaiming its superiority to both English, which he considered a weak, courtly, 'invented language', and French; Scots on the other hand was natural, bold, 'firy' and was spoken by both the 'commons' and 'men of Busynesse'.

There was a darker side to Restoration society. The middle of the seventeenth century saw hysteria on the subject of alleged witchcraft reach a new intensity. It had begun during the wars. The theocracy found accusations of witchcraft to its taste; they were, apart from other considerations, a means of keeping the populace obedient. In the summer of 1649, for instance, more than 350 individual commissions to investigate witchcraft were issued, mostly in East Lothian and Berwickshire. Between 1657 and 1659 there were 102 witchcraft trials. Three hundred alleged or self-confessed witches were put to death in 1661–2. The

number of unfortunates burnt for witchcraft far exceeded the sum of the Covenanting martyrs. Only gradually did the temper change and the zeal for denunciation moderate. Mackenzie called the 'witch prickers' 'villainous cheats'.

One case took on a wider and more sinister significance. Thomas Weir, from a Lanarkshire family, was a soldier known for his conspicuous and exemplary piety. He had served in Ireland in the army sent by the Scottish Covenanting estates to help suppress the Catholic Rising of 1641, and was subsequently captain of the Edinburgh Town Guard, in charge of the arrangements for Montrose's imprisonment before execution, in which capacity he allowed his troopers to fill the prisoner's room with tobacco smoke, which the marquess loathed. His Calvinism was extreme; it was said that if three or four of the strictest Presbyterians were gathered together, Major Weir was sure to be one of them. He was a grim-looking fellow with a big nose and was never seen without his staff, to which magical properties were to be attributed. He never married, but lived in the West Bow with his sister Grizel; at the prayer meetings held there his power of extempore prayer filled all with admiration. He was given the sobriquet 'Angelical Thomas'.

There was, therefore, consternation when, having fallen sick, he suddenly confessed, voluntarily and, it would seem, without prompting, to consort with the devil and other 'crimes of the most revolting nature', according to an account offered by the Reverend Mr Fraser, minister of Wardlaw, in his *Divine Providences* (1670). Though Weir admitted his guilt, he refused to beg pardon from the Almighty, responding to every plea with the words, uttered in a scream, 'Torment me no more – I am tormented enough already.' His confession seemed so incredible that the Provost, Sir Allan Ramsay, at first refused to take him into custody, but at last it was believed; the major was tried, sentenced to death and burnt in the Grassmarket. The famous staff, thrown into the fire also, 'gave rare turnings and was long a-burning, as also himself'. He had refused the consolations of religion even up to the end, crying out, 'Let me alone – I will not – I have lived as a beast, and I must die as a beast.'

His wretched sister, who was crazy as a coot, was hanged. She had claimed that her mother had also been a witch. 'The secretest thing,' she said, 'that I, or any of the family could do, when once a mark appeared on her brow, she could tell it them, though done at a great distance.' This mark could, she claimed, also appear on her own forehead whenever she chose. To prove it, she pushed back her head-dress 'and there', the author of *Satan's Invisible World Discovered* assures us, 'was an exact horse-shoe shaped for nails in her wrinkles, terrible enough, I assure you, to the stoutest beholder.' And so indeed it must have been, if of course you believed in that sort of thing.

But many did. The major became a legend. In the tale of diablerie which Scott has the blind fiddler tell in *Redgauntlet*, in which the fiddler's grandfather has to go down into Hell to recover a receipt from his master Sir Robert Redgauntlet, one of the many persecutors of the godly, Sir Robert has an ape called Major Weir. Weir's house in the West Bow was long left empty, believed to be haunted. When some fifty years later it was at last occupied, the new tenants were driven from it in terror after 'a form like that of a calf' had appeared in their chamber and placed its fore-hooves on the bed. Clearly the devil still claimed the place as his own. For a long time it was known that certain citizens of Edinburgh sometimes saw the major emerge from the close at night, mounted on a black horse without a head, and then gallop off into the mirk, to keep a tryst with his infernal master. On other occasions the empty house was seen at night to be illuminated, and sounds of music, dancing, howling and, oddly, spinning, could be heard.

The story is grotesque, horrible of course, yet not easy to dismiss. The fanatical religiosity of seventeenth-century Scotland, with its insistence on damnation from which the Elect were spared only by God's Grace, could easily topple into a species of dementia, in which the Elect could persuade themselves that anything was permitted to those assured of salvation. Weir was no doubt what in ordinary eyes would seem a complete hypocrite; yet it was but a step, as John Buchan suggests in *Witch Wood*, from one extreme to another. The fullest expression of this state of mind is offered by James Hogg in his masterpiece *The Private Memoirs and Confessions of a Justified Sinner*. This novel, written in the early nineteenth century but set at the turn of the seventeenth and eighteenth, explores the state of mind that made such as Major Weir possible. The hero, or anti-hero, encounters the devil at the very moment when he has received assurance of

being among the Elect, as he looks down 'with pity and contempt on the grovelling creatures below'. Consumed with pride, he is powerless to resist the temptations of evil, which cannot harm him on account of his exalted state. 'To the wicked all things are wicked; but to the just all things are just and right.'

Deacon Brodie
by John Kay, 1788

opposite
Figure of Death from a late 17th-century memorial in Greyfriars Churchyard
(the monument of James Borthwick, 1676)

The duality of Edinburgh's nature has often been remarked on. For some it finds expression in the sharp contrast between the Old Town, with its Gothic mystery, and the New Town shining lucid in Attic light. For others it is incarnated in the history of eighteenth-century Deacon Brodie, magistrate by day and thief by night, who was eventually hanged on a gallow of his own construction. Brodie fascinated Stevenson, and *The Strange Case of Dr Jekyll and Mr Hyde*, Stevenson's exploration of the theme of duality, owes something to his interest in Brodie. But the double nature preceded the building of the New Town, and Brodie is a dull figure compared to Major Weir, his crimes modest and fully comprehensible. It is Weir and the hero of Hogg's novel who strike the authentic note of the Divided Self.

5

The Union and its Consequences

The revolution of 1688 was generally welcomed in Lowland Scotland. The Presbyterian Church was re-established, episcopacy again abolished, and the ministers who had accepted the Restoration Church settlement driven from their manses – 'rabbled' was the contemporary expression. Henceforth, surviving Episcopalians were to be Jacobites, longing for the return of the Stewarts. They were patriots, but out of tune with the majority of their fellow-countrymen, south of Aberdeenshire and the Highland Line at least.

View of Edinburgh from the Nor' Loch by John Slezer, late 17th century

Nevertheless, those who looked forward to a new Golden Age were to be disappointed, just as those who feared the return of the bigoted theocracy were mistaken. The new Church establishment was mellower and more moderate; the religious temper had cooled somewhat. Soon, the suffering Saints of the Covenant would secede from a Church they deemed lukewarm, Laodicean, even Erastian.

The 1690s were a wretched decade, a time of poor harvests and even famine: Fletcher of Saltoun guessed that one in five of the population died. Edinburgh was sorely affected also by the war with France, which curtailed its traditional trade with the Continent. Then the most ambitious commercial venture yet in Scottish history proved disastrous. This was the Darien Scheme, promoted as a means of curing the nation's economic ills. Landowners all over Scotland invested heavily in the 'Company of Scotland trading to Africa and the Indies', but the main investors, and losers, were the financiers and merchants of Edinburgh and the east coast burghs who had helped found the Bank of Scotland in 1695. The two expeditions sent to found a colony on the Isthmus of Darien were fiascos. The company itself collapsed in 1700. The hostility of the English court, of the City of London and of Spain was blamed; but in truth, though there was some substance in the charges levelled at William III and his English ministers, the ruined investors were the victims of their own folly and unfounded optimism. Nevertheless, this failure, though it aroused animosity against England, also persuaded some that only through union could Scotland hope to attain prosperity. It is not therefore surprising that fifteen of the twenty-five Articles of Union eventually prepared in 1706 were concerned with economics.

The immediate cause of the union was more narrowly political, born of the English fear, in the midst of the French War, that Scotland would choose to separate herself completely from England when the now childless Queen Anne died, and choose a different monarch who might well be the Jacobite pretender, Anne's Catholic half-brother James Stewart. Certainly that was the hope and intention of the still strong Jacobite party in Scotland, which therefore bitterly opposed the projected union.

The same fear of a Jacobite restoration agitated many Scots; they might dislike the idea of union with England and the consequent loss of national independence, but they disliked the alternative more. For it was clear that England would not acquiesce in a Jacobite restoration in Scotland: the prospect of another English invasion loomed, only half a century after Cromwell had forced Scotland into union. Whatever happened, Presbyterians and Whigs could not believe it would be good. Either there would be a Stewart restoration, in which case they feared to lose all they had gained by the settlement of 1688–9, or there would be renewed war with England with all the danger that threatened. Many accordingly found themselves dragged unwillingly by the force of logic towards accepting a negotiated union. It was the least of evils, and so they acquiesced, many of the nobility softening the blow by accepting bribes and the promise of preferment in office or condition from the English Government. There were some sincere enthusiasts for union, like the Lord Provost of Edinburgh, Sir Patrick Johnston, and the Earl of Cromarty, but they were rare.

That the union was generally unpopular there can be no doubt. Relations between Scotland and England had been embittered by the Darien experience, and this was exacerbated by subsequent events. The Aliens Act passed in Westminster in 1703, which threatened to treat all Scots, except those already domiciled in England, as aliens, and to ban trade between the two kingdoms, may have been intended to persuade Scots of the virtue of union, but its immediate effect was quite the contrary. The mood in Scotland, and in Edinburgh in particular, was demonstrated when an English ship, the *Worcester*, was seized in the Firth of Forth by agents of the Company of Scotland who claimed the right to confiscate its cargo as compensation for their losses. Its unfortunate Captain Green then found himself charged with piracy, and was executed in Edinburgh on 11 April 1705, with the Scottish Privy Council carefully averting its eyes from this example of judicial murder.

But if the mood was hot against union, it was also confused. Sir John Clerk of Penicuik, Member of Parliament for Whithorn and a member also of one of the greatest dynasties of the Scots bar, a Whig who favoured union, analysed the contradictions in the opposition attitudes:

> Here you may find several persons exalting a union of confederacy [as opposed to the Incorporating Union which England had come to demand], and at the same time exclaiming against that article of the treaty concerning equal duties, customs, and excises, as if there could be a union of confederacy . . . without equal burdens . . . Others quarrell with the charges the nation will be put to in sending up sixteen Peers and forty-five Commons to the parliament of Great Britain, and at the same time, both in words and writings, they cry out against that number as a small, dishonourable representation. Some are regretting the extream poverty of the nation and scarcity of money; yet, notwithstanding, they exclaim against the Union as a thing that will ruin us; not considering how any condition of life we can fall into, can render us more miserable and poor than we are . . . In a corner of the street you may see a Presbyterian minister, a Popish priest, and an Episcopal prelate, all agreeing in their discourse against the Union, but upon quite different views and contradictory reasons.

Clerk thought such arguments evidence of 'the triumph in our streets' of 'wilful ignorance, contradiction and inconsistencies'. So no doubt they were; similar ignorance, contradictions and inconsistencies may be found at any time in the three centuries since.

Whatever Clerk's cool logic might produce as an argument in favour of union, it failed to persuade the people of Edinburgh. Lockhart of Carnwath, as a Jacobite, is as prejudiced a witness of the case against the union as Clerk was for it, but his account, however partisan, gives a vivid impression of the popular mood in the capital:

> During this time, the Nation's Aversion to the Union increased; the Parliament Close, and the outer Parliament House, were crowded every Day when the Parliament was met, with an infinite Number of People, all exclaiming against the Union, and speaking very free Language concerning the Promoters of it. The Commissioner, as he passed along the street, was cursed

and reviled to his Face, and the Duke of Hamilton
huzza'd and convey'd every Night, with a great Number
of Apprentices and younger Sort of People, from the
Parliament House to the Abbey, exhorting him to stand
by the Country and assuring him of being supported.
And upon the Twenty Third of October [1706] above
Three or Four Hundred of them being thus employ'd,
did, as soon as they left his Grace, hasten in a Body to the
House of Sir Pat Johnston (their late darling Provost, one
of the Commissioners of the Treaty, a great Promoter of
the Union, in Parliament, where he sat as one of the
representatives of the Town of Edinburgh,) threw Stones
at his Windows, broke open his Doors, and search'd his
House for him, but he having narrowly made his Escape,
prevented his being torn in a Thousand Pieces. From
thence the Mob, which was encreas'd to a great Number,
went thro' the Streets, threatning Destruction on all the
Promoters of the Union, and continu'd for four or five
Hours in this Temper; till about three next Morning, a
strong Detachment of the Foot Guards was sent to secure
the Gate call'd the Netherbow Port, and keep Guard in
the Parliament Close.

Daniel Defoe, in Edinburgh as an agent of the English government, told the same story to his master, Robert Harley, the
Secretary of State for the Northern Department. Defoe 'heard a
Great Noise and looking out saw a Terrible Multitude Come up
the High Street with a Drum at the head of Them shouting and
swearing and Cryeing out all Scotland would stand together, No
Union, No Union, English Dogs, and the like'. Nevertheless he
judged, like Clerk of Penicuik, that 'there is an Entire Harmony in
This Country Consisting in Universall Discords'.

   These months when Scotland's capital was for the last time a
true centre of national politics were therefore confused. That
there was little enthusiasm for the union, even among its
promoters, is certain; they saw it as only the best way out of a
nasty mess. Perhaps the proposals could have been defeated if
the opposition had been united in anything but its dislike of the
treaty. But since one wing of the opposition disliked and
distrusted the other wing, even more than it disliked and
distrusted the treaty, and since moderate men in the middle
feared nothing so much as the civil war or the war with England

which rejection of the treaty might lead to, the thing went
through, the fierce hostility of the mobs in Edinburgh, Glasgow
and other towns and cities in the end counting for nothing.

There is a tradition that on 1 May 1707, the day the union was
made real, somebody gained access to the bells of the High Kirk
of St Giles and rang out the old tune 'How Can I Be Sad Upon My
Wedding Day?' If it is not true, it is at least a good invention, for
'the tradition reflects,' as David Daiches has written, 'an ambival-
ence of feeling about the Union that is found in Scotland again
and again after 1707. This ambiguity,' he adds, 'is seen in both
Burns and Scott,' each of them capable in different moods of
expressing either a British patriotism or an even more powerful,
perhaps, Scottish national feeling and resentment. For there can
be no doubt that whatever was gained in 1707 – and the gains
were real, material and significant – something vital was also lost,
a certain self-respect and self-assurance, so that in the generations since we have often alternated uneasily between nostalgia
and bluster.

To admit this is not to say that the union was a mistake, or
ought to be ended, for whatever it took away, it gave Scotland a
political security the country had never enjoyed, and that security at
the very least contributed to the remarkable efflorescence of
learning, imagination, enterprise and industry that distinguished the next century and a half. There is much argument,
largely and inevitably inconclusive, as to whether the Scottish
Enlightenment was the result of the union or whether its causes
can be discerned in pre-union Scotland. The argument *post hoc
propter hoc* is never satisfactory, though in a sense of course it is
true that everything which happens after a certain event in time is
to some extent, locally, a consequence of it. We cannot tell how
Scotland would have developed had the union been rejected; we
know only how things turned out within the union; and so the
union must at the very least be given some credit for the
achievements of eighteenth- and nineteenth-century Scotland,
just as the failures of that society cannot be divorced from the
working of the union either.

It is, however, at least possible that the decay of politics within
Scotland – the strange decades of political lassitude that lay

between the decline of Jacobitism and the rise of the demand for Parliamentary reform – contributed to the flowering of the Enlightenment. No longer agitated by political strife, men turned their minds to questions of social and economic improvement and the pleasures of philosophy and history. The dual awareness of what had been lost and of the possibilities now open to Scotsmen created an intellectual tension which found release in the achievements of the Enlightenment, especially in Edinburgh.

It was the loss that was felt first. The importance of the capital was diminished, and the people felt the decline in status and influence. In *The Heart of Midlothian*, Scott has an old woman say, 'When we had a king, and a chancellor, and parliament-men o' our ain, we could aye peeble them wi' stanes when they werna gude bairns – But naebody's nails can reach the length of Lunnon.' Scottish politics had always been intimate. The people crowded round the gates of Holyrood and the Parliament Close itself; classes mixed higgledy-piggledy in the tall lands of the High Street and the dank narrow closes than ran off it. Now power was remote; it seemed as if London had eaten up Edinburgh.

A macabre story told of the very day when the union was made seemed to prefigure this. No nobleman had had more influence on the passing of the measure than James, second Duke of Queensberry. Now it happened that his eldest son, James, Lord Drumlanrig, was an idiot, of uncontrollable temper and appetites, and also unusually tall, as the size of his coffin in the family vault at Durisdeer is said to prove. There had always been a strain of ferocity in the Douglas blood, and in this unfortunate it took a monstrous shape. When the family were in Edinburgh, he was usually confined in a wing of Queensberry House in the Canongate, with the windows boarded up so that the poor wretch could neither see nor be seen. On the day the union was passed, the whole household went to Parliament Close, such was the general excitement; and the lunatic's keeper went with them. His charge escaped from his confinement, roamed round the deserted house and found his way to the kitchen. The only person there was a boy turning the spit on which the dinner was roasting. Lord Drumlanrig apparently killed the boy, removed the meat from the fire and substituted his victim on the spit. When the duke returned in triumph from Parliament House, he discovered his son consuming his ghastly meal. The common people said it was God's judgement on the duke for his part in the wickedness of the union.

One consequence of the union is often said to have been the departure of the nobility from Edinburgh, as they were drawn south by the two magnets of court and Parliament. To some extent this happened, but the case can be exaggerated. Even sixty years later many of the houses in the Canongate were occupied by members of the old landed and noble interest. Chambers in his invaluable *Traditions of Edinburgh* gives a list of those resident there, as recalled by a certain Mr Chalmers Izett 'whose memory extended back to 1769'. It contains two dukes (Queensberry and Hamilton), sixteen earls, two countesses, seven other lords (not counting seven Lords of Session who were naturally obliged to reside in Edinburgh) and more than a dozen baronets. Moreover, when the New Town was built, many nobles had town houses there. The Secretary of State's official residence, Bute House in Charlotte Square, is one such.

The Edinburgh mob, thwarted at the time of the union, was to have one last hideous triumph. It was then the custom for men condemned to death to be made to attend Church the Sunday before their execution in order that they might be brought to a proper state of mind before they were called to account by their Maker. On one such occasion, in the late winter of 1736, a condemned prisoner contrived to escape from his guards in the Tolbooth Kirk. (He made his way down the back stairs into the Cowgate, and then was heard of no more till he arrived in Holland.) His companion, however, was restrained by the guards, and brought to execution at the appointed time. His case had aroused a good deal of sympathy, partly because it was thought that he had assisted his friend's escape, and it was therefore rather unfair that he should hang alone; partly because he was a smuggler, and Sir Robert Walpole's Excise Bill had made that activity even more generally popular than previously. At any rate the mood was such that the authorities expected trouble, and

*The port of the Abbey of
Holyrood, with a view of the
Canongate*
by Paul Sandby

the scaffold was guarded by an unusually large detachment of troops, three or four companies of an infantry regiment being brought in to support the City Guard which was commanded by a Captain Porteous, a man already deeply disliked by the Edinburgh mob. No attempt at rescue was made, and the prisoner was hanged. At that moment some of the crowd started throwing stones and dung at the hangman. In the opinion of one observer, the Reverend Alexander Carlyle of Inveresk, 'there was little, if any, more violence than was usually offered on such occasions. Porteous, however, inflamed with wine and jealousy, thought proper to order his guards to fire.' Some aimed over the heads of the crowd, unfortunately killing a spectator in the upper window of the house opposite. Eight or nine people were left dead when the crowd dispersed.

Porteous was arrested and found guilty of murder. He was reprieved from death, however, to the fury of the mob. They stormed the Tolbooth Prison where he was confined, and dragged him from a chimney where he was hiding. Then, moving with absolute order and in strict discipline, they carried him down to the Grassmarket, pausing to break open a rope-maker's shop in the West Bow, and reputedly leaving a guinea as payment for the rope they took, 'so anxious', Scott writes in *The Heart of Midlothian*, 'were the perpetrators of this daring action to show that they meditated not the slightest wrong or infraction of the law, excepting so far as Porteous himself was concerned'. Since the gibbet had been removed, and was stored in the basement of Parliament House, where it lay between terms of duty, they hanged the wretched man from a dyester's pole.

The discipline of the mob has been much commended, and they may have performed justice of a sort; but it was nevertheless lynch law, which their discipline may indeed be thought to render more, rather than less, terrible. The government was furious, the City Council was suspended, rewards for information were offered, but no one came forward and the deed went unpunished.

Nine years later Edinburgh for a few months again put on the appearance of a national capital. The Jacobite Romance of the '45 broke into the Age of Reason with a wholly alarming irrationality, and for a few weeks Reason trembled. At first the City Council was determined to resist the prince and his Highland army (even though the Lord Provost, Sir Archibald Stewart, was suspected of Jacobite sympathies), but when they learned that the Hanoverian army commanded by Sir John Cope was prepared to come no nearer than Leith, their enthusiasm diminished. More than four hundred men of a volunteer force had taken up position at the gates on the morning of 16 September, but by noon scarcely more than forty remained at their chosen post. (One of them was the great philosopher and historian David Hume.)

The castle was held by government troops, but they made no move, and the detachment of Jacobites commanded by Cameron of Lochiel entered Edinburgh by the Netherbow Port. Meanwhile the main body of the army marched by way of Merchiston and Hope's Park, out of range of the castle guns, to the little glen called the Hunter's Bog between Arthur's Seat and the Salisbury Crags. Here, about midday on the 17th, 'Bonnie' Prince Charlie rode along a bridle path to St Anthony's Well where he gazed over Holyrood and gave a growing crowd the first sight of the son of their hereditary monarch.

One observer was John Home, who later wrote a History of the Rebellion. He saw that 'the figure and presence of Charles Stuart were not ill-suited to his lofty pretensions. He was in the prime of youth, tall and handsome, of a fair complexion; he had a light coloured periwig with his own hair combed over the front: he wore the Highland dress, that is a tartan short coat without the plaid, a blue bonnet on his head, and on his breast the star of the order of St Andrew. Charles stood some time in the park to shew himself to the people; and then, though he was very near the palace, mounted his horse, either to render himself more conspicuous, or because he rode well and looked graceful on horseback.'

He dismounted at the gate of the palace and was conducted within by James Hepburn of Keith, who had been out in the '15 and for thirty years 'had kept himself in constant readiness to take arms'. That afternoon the prince's absent father (living in exile in Rome) was proclaimed 'James VIII and III, King of Scotland, England, France and Ireland' and Charles his regent, at

Prince Charles Edward Stewart
after Maurice Quentin de la
Tour

the Mercat Cross, by a somewhat reluctant City Herald who had
been routed from his hiding place by Lochiel. The ceremony was
decorated by the appearance of Mrs Murray of Broughton, wife of
the prince's secretary who, mounted on a white horse and
sporting the white cockade, took up position by the cross with a
drawn sword in her hand.

A few days later the army marched out by way of Duddingston to the East Lothian coast where Sir John Cope's army was scattered in a quarter of an hour after the autumn sunrise. 'They eskaped like rabets,' the prince informed his father. Then he returned to Edinburgh where he forbade any public celebration of the victory saying he was 'far from rejoicing at the death of any of his father's Subjects'. (After Culloden the Hanoverians would take rather a different view of such matters.)

Then, for a few weeks, while preparations were made for the invasion of England (despite the prince's proclamation that the pretended union between the two kingdoms was now annulled), Holyrood played the part of a royal palace for which it was intended, a role it has so seldom filled.

6

The Age of Improvement

For all its glamour and pathos, the Jacobite Rising was no more than an interlude, an operatic diversion from the steady course of Edinburgh's history in the eighteenth century. That century, the most glorious in the city's career, has been called the Age of Reason; to the men of the time it was pre-eminently the Age of Improvement. Scotland enjoyed a prolonged, unprecedented peace. Apart from the '45, there was freedom from civil strife. Equally important there was freedom from factional conflict, and even the wars of the theologians were muted and took on a new gentleness. There were neither political murders nor the judicial execution of failed politicians, if again we make an exception for the Jacobite victims. The nobility lived without fear. They no longer needed to fortify their country houses, and they busied themselves either in attempts to secure political preferment, through assiduous cultivation of the ministries, or in improving their estates.

The same tranquillity distinguished Edinburgh. Though there was still a general agreement as to the truth and importance of the Christian religion – David Hume was a rare, if notable, dissenter from this view – nevertheless men were now more concerned to cultivate their intellect than to tend their souls. It was therefore a time when great numbers of social bodies came into being, all devoted to improvements of one kind or another. Edinburgh remained an aristocratic city; the landed interest controlled the patronage of the Church and supplied the membership of the Faculty of Advocates: the two institutional focal points of the city's life. It was within this orbit that the various

'The Clubbists':
engraving by Raddon after
David Wilkie

clubs and societies flourished. They all had the same aim: to draw men with literary, philosophical, scientific and speculative tastes together so that members could explore ideas and try their theories against each other's intellects. The two best known were The Honourable Society for Improvement of Knowledge of Agriculture (fl. 1723–45), which from this apparently narrow base acquired a general interest in questions of political economy, and the Select Society (1754–63), whose founders included Hume, Adam Smith, Allan Ramsay and the Reverend Alexander 'Jupiter' Carlyle; its discussions ranged over the whole spectrum of human affairs: politics, economics, morals and the improvement of manners. Like the Agricultural Society, it attracted noblemen, but within the Society they had to take second place to the distinguished intellectuals. It has been suggested (by Norman Phillipson) that 'the social and ideological links these two societies have with the old Scots parliaments allow us to think of them as para-parliaments designed to demonstrate that political leadership still lay in the hands of a traditional governing class'. Yet the manifest tendency to consider every question open to discussion, and every custom open to improvement, logically called that very concept into question. The implications of the spirit of free-ranging enquiry were to impose great strains on Scottish society at the end of the century.

This was not apparent in the first years of the union. Then, even those whose political principles inclined them to oppose the union, contributed to the new sense of intellectual adventure. Thomas Ruddiman (1674–1757), for instance, was an ardent Jacobite, being an Episcopalian from the north-east. But he had been appointed Assistant Keeper of the Advocates' Library in 1700, becoming Principal Keeper in 1727, a post he held till his death. He had also set up as a printer or publisher about the time of the union, and was therefore a central figure in Edinburgh's intellectual life. He was a founder of at least two clubs, the Easy Club and the Rankenian (1716). The latter was a philosophical society, whose members carried on a correspondence with Bishop Berkeley; his 'Principles of Human Knowledge' had been published in 1710 and within twenty years students at Edinburgh University were being set essays on Berkeley's work, then unknown, or despised and disregarded, at Oxford and Cambridge.

Thomas Ruddiman
by William Denune, 1749

Ruddiman was an important link between seventeenth- and eighteenth-century Scotland. He also, in his own work and person, serves to illustrate the dilemma in which Scottish society found itself, a dilemma that would grow still more urgent as the century progressed, and the influence of the union was more powerfully felt. In 1755 the *Edinburgh Review* (the first of a number of magazines to have that title) declared,

> The communication of trade has awakened industry; the
> equal administration of laws produced good manners;
> and the watchful care of the government, seconded by
> the public spirit of some individuals, has excited,
> promoted, and encouraged a disposition to every species
> of improvement in the minds of a people naturally active
> and intelligent. If countries have their ages in respect to
> improvement, North Britain may be considered in a state
> of early youth, guided and supported by the mature state
> of her kindred country.

Many would have agreed with these sentiments, and even
patriotic Scotsmen like David Hume took great care to remove
Scotticisms from their written language – in the interest of
civilised manners.

Yet there was also a profound and lively consciousness that
Scotland was a nation with a proud and sturdily independent
history, and that the sense of identity which this had nourished
was threatened by the very improvements of which, in other
moods, Scotsmen might be equally proud. So the zeal for
progress in the refinements of civilisation existed alongside a
keen nostalgia for the Scotland that was passing away. It was as
much a patriotic duty to rescue that Scotland from the oblivion
that menaced it as it was to work for improvements. Very often
the same people were animated by both sentiments; some of the
mental and moral energy they displayed was the consequence of
the tensions set up by their dual consciousness of Scotland as an
independent and historic nation with a distinct culture, and
Scotland as a partner in the enterprise of creating a Greater
Britain.

Ruddiman may again be taken as an early exemplar of this
duality. His publication of Gavin Douglas's translation of *The
Aeneid* and his edition of the complete Latin works of Buchanan
(with an introduction by himself severely critical of Buchanan's
views of the Reformation and of monarchy) testified to his
sympathy with Renaissance Scotland; his publication of Colin
McLaurin (1698–1746), post-Newtonian mathematician and
astronomer, to his sympathy with the new.

Allan Ramsay the Elder, a friend of Ruddiman and member
of his Easy Club, attempted a synthesis of the inherited tradition

with present realities, and did so with a surer popular touch. Born in 1686 in Dumfriesshire, the son of the factor to the estates there of the great legal dynasty of the Hopes of Hopetoun, Ramsay was first apprenticed to an Edinburgh wigmaker. (By 1700 there were sixty-five wigmakers in the city.) In 1719 he set up as a bookseller, and nine years later opened Edinburgh's first

The Bibliophilists' Haunt
(Creech's Bookshop)
by Sir William Fettes Douglas

circulating library. His poems were published by the Easy Club, and in 1724 he brought out the first volume of an anthology of old and new Scots songs. His most significant work, however, was his pastoral ballad-opera 'The Gentle Shepherd'. Set in rural Scotland (much influenced by Arcadian ideas) some thirty years before his birth, it drew also on Augustan sources, being imbued with the moral teaching of Addison, Steele and Arbuthnott, the last two of whom had subscribed, along with Pope and John Gay, to Ramsay's first collection of verses. 'The Gentle Shepherd' was an intelligent and sensitive attempt to achieve a harmony between the world that had passed away and that which had come into being. It suggested that Scots need not lose their sense of being Scottish while acquiring the new British identity. When Ramsay's son, also called Allan, the greatest portrait painter of the mid-century, became Court Painter to George III, the synthesis was complete.

The brightest star in the firmament of Edinburgh intellectuals was David Hume, a native of the city, though from a family of Berwickshire lairds. Hume was pure philosopher, historian and political economist. He did more than anyone to form the theory that lay behind what has been called the Scotch Science of Man. His philosophy enabled men to make sense of the world and of human society in purely human terms. He banished metaphysics and theology from philosophical discussion of moral and social conduct; and what he had to say about the sympathetic mechanisms which order our social relations made it possible for philosophers to consider how a society might be held together by cultural, and not merely political, bonds. These ideas had a special force in Scotland, as a society which had recently acquiesced in the resignation of its political independence and the devaluation of its political structures, without surrendering its sense of itself as being distinct.

Hume's historical work marked a new advance. He believed that society developed, unconsciously, through stages each characterised by a different economic structure. (In this he anticipated Marx.) His theory allowed therefore for the natural involuntary progress which came about through the clash of opposing forces, the outcome reflecting the character of both parties in the quarrel. This theory of history was neither facile nor necessarily optimistic, for he realised that a relapse into barbarism was as possible as an advance to a higher level of civilisation, but his insistence that society could not be intelligently studied without reference to social structures not only contributed to the deepening of historiography, but enabled his compatriots to understand the present condition of Scotland. He set the pattern for the philosophical historians of the second half of the century – Robertson, Ferguson and Millar – whose writings did so much to form the way in which Sir Walter Scott strove to understand the past and its enduring influence on the present.

Hume's thought was rarefied, difficult, despite the lucidity of his language; it took a long time to percolate. Meanwhile, however, more practical improvements were transforming Edinburgh. The first Assembly Rooms were opened in the West Bow in 1711, and though they were, as Chambers puts it, 'held in abhorrence by the Presbyterians and only struggled through a desultory and degraded existence by the favour of the Jacobites, who have always been a less strait-laced part of the community', they survived as evidence of a new regard for the cultivation of genteel manners.

By 1720 Edinburgh had two newspapers. Then George Drummond in his first term as Lord Provost in 1725 drew up plans for a new medical school: the Medical Society was founded in 1731. By the end of the century four hundred of the eleven hundred students at the University were studying medicine; an American student called it 'the first University in Europe for medicine', a reputation it would long maintain.

The city itself was expanding, even though the growth of population, from about 50,000 in 1700 to 75,000 by 1770, was slower than that of either Glasgow or Aberdeen. Plans for expansion actually went back to the 1680s, encouraged by James VII, but these were thwarted by the revolution and the misery of the 1690s. In 1720, however, the City Council bought the Loch Bank estate, on the far side of the Nor' Loch under the Castle Rock, ground now covered by Princes Street and George Street. Nothing further was done at the time, and the city's first expansion was to the south, though James Court, north of the Lawnmarket but still on the Old City side of the loch, was built in 1727 by James Brownhill, who appealed to prospective customers by supplying a private scavenging service to improve the amenities of the court. But the pressures for expansion could not be contained within the old walls; George Square to the south was composed of decent stone houses in a vernacular style. ('No architect of standing defends George Square,' announced those modern luminaries Sir Robert Matthew and Sir Basil Spence in 1959 when the University proposed its destruction. Two sides of the square were accordingly pulled down, to be brutally replaced.)

By the time George Square was completed plans were already afoot to build the New Town on the open ground to the north. 'Proposals for carrying on certain Public Works in the City of Edinburgh' had been drawn up in 1752 by Gilbert Elliott, the future Lord Minto. They were probably inspired by Drummond, the visionary of the new Edinburgh. There were four chief proposals: to build an Exchange upon the ruins on the north side of the High Street. This was done in 1753, but was never popular with merchants, and the City Chambers now stand where the Exchange used to be. Second, 'to erect upon the ruins in Parliament Close, a building for the law courts, the town council, "several registers", the advocates' library'. Third, to obtain an Act of Parliament extending the city's royalty; to enlarge and beautify the town by opening new streets to the north and south, removing the markets and the shambles, and turning the North Loch into a canal with walks and terraces on either side. Fourth, to defray the expenses of this work by a public subscription.

View to the northwest from a roof-top on the north side of the High Street, c. 1750 (anon.): looking towards the site of the New Town; Corstorphine Hill and the settlement of Drumsheugh are visible in the distance

These proposals contained the germ of the most ambitious piece of town planning. The Nor' Loch was drained, and in 1763 the building of the North Bridge across the ravine began. (Part of it collapsed six years later, killing half a dozen people.) By that time, however, a competition for the design of the New Town

'A View of the New Bridge of Edinburgh . . . from the West': engraving by Thomas Donaldson

James Craig's Plan of the New Town, 1767

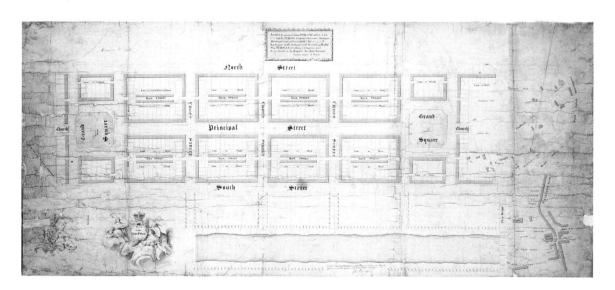

had been launched, and won by an unknown twenty-two-year-old architect, James Craig. What is called the first New Town, extending as far north as Queen Street, is essentially Craig's design, though the circus he planned for the middle of George Street, to complement the squares at either end, was never built.

The New Town was not absolutely uniform even from the start. The plan that two churches should face each other along the length of George Street was foiled when Sir William Chambers, architect of Somerset House in London, was commissioned by Sir Lawrence Dundas to build a mansion where it was intended that St Andrew's Church should stand; it is now the head office of the Royal Bank of Scotland, and St Andrew's was relegated to the north side of George Street. David Hume was one of the first to move to the New Town, building himself a house on the corner of St Andrew's Square. Since the short street linking the square to Princes Street had not yet been named, the philosopher, famous for his lack of religion and suspected of atheism, got a workman to paint the name 'St David's Street' on the corner of his house. If the story is not true, it is nicely imagined.

Building started at the east end. Evidence of confidence in the plan was afforded by the construction of Register House,

Register House (elevation of south front): drawing by Robert Adam

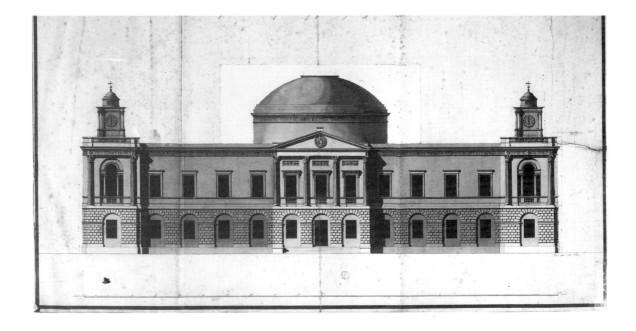

designed by the Adam brothers, Robert and James, to face up the North Bridge. It was funded by the government from the sale of forfeited Jacobite estates. Robert Adam was also to be responsible for the design of Charlotte Square at the West End of the New Town. Even so, his masterpiece in Edinburgh is the Old College of the University on South Bridge. The narrowness of the street means that the casual passer-by easily remains ignorant of its magnificence. This, however, adds to the sense that Edinburgh is a truly European city, for many grand palazzi in Rome or Naples rise from similarly mean streets and do not disclose their splendour at first glance.

The style of the New Town was carefully controlled by the imposition of strict feu conditions. The result is more apparent today in what came to be called the Second New Town, built to the north and down the hill from the first. Commercial development long ago destroyed the homogeneity of Princes Street and George Street, even of St Andrew's Square; but in the second New Town Gillespie Graham's magnificent Moray Place provides evidence of what such control of individual taste could achieve.

Moray Place: engraving after Thomas Shepherd

In one important respect the New Town preserved a characteristic of the Old. Most of the houses were tenemented, even if this is rarely apparent from the street. The Scots still preserved a taste for living in flats. In any case, though the country was growing richer, there were few Edinburgh citizens who could have afforded to maintain a whole five- or six-storey house.

The New Town aroused mixed feelings from the start. Cockburn's account of its extension is characteristic:

> It was about this time that the Earl of Moray's ground to the north of Charlotte Square began to be broken up for being built on. It was then an open field of as green turf as Scotland could boast of, with a few respectable trees on the flat, and thickly wooded on the bank along the water of Leith. Moray Place and Ainslie Place stand there now. It was the beginning of a sad change, as we felt then. That well-kept and almost evergreen field was the most beautiful piece of ground in immediate connection with the town, and led the eye agreeably over to our distant northern scenery. How glorious the prospect on a summer evening, from Queen Street! We had got into the habit of believing that the mere charm of the ground to us would keep it sacred, and were inclined to cling to our conviction even after we saw the foundations digging. We then thought with despair of our lost verdure, our banished peacefulness, our gorgeous sunsets. But it was unavoidable. We would never have got beyond the North Loch, if these feelings had been conclusive. But how can I forget the glory of that scene! on the still nights in which, with Rutherford and Richardson and Jeffrey, I have stood in Queen Street, or the opening at the north-west corner of Charlotte Square, and listened to the ceaseless rural corn-craiks, nestling happily in the dewy grass. It would be some consolation if the buildings were worthy of the situation, but the northern houses are turned the wrong way, and everything is sacrificed to the multiplication of feuing feet.

Cockburn was a complicated man, as we shall see; too despondent, also, for the view over the Firth of Forth from Queen Street still affords a glorious prospect, and Moray Place is handsome whatever he says, still the most desirable address in Edinburgh, even though the houses on the north side only look to the Forth from their kitchens and back bedrooms. Now that people no longer have servants they perhaps feel this deprivation less than Cockburn did.

But Ruskin agreed with him about the architecture of the New Town, condemning its austere uniformity, deploring the 678 plain and identical windows of Queen Street, 'altogether void of any relief by decoration . . . I cannot say that it is entertaining.'

Stevenson, as we shall see, was a great admirer of the New Town, at a time when it had become fashionable to condemn it. Time has confirmed his judgement. The New Town is generally appreciated and subject to strict rules of conservation. Ironically, as will be seen, it was the Cockburn Association which ensured that it would not be despoiled.

Another allegation, more serious perhaps, was levelled against it, one that still surfaces as criticism today. The Old Town, it is argued, correctly, was a hiddledy-piggledy, socially hetero-geneous place; the building of the New Town introduced a species of social apartheid to Edinburgh. Gradually the Old Town was abandoned to the poor, while the prosperous bourgeoisie ensconced themselves in the sedate squares and bland streets of the New. An American who visited the city in 1834 remarked that 'Paris is not more unlike Constantinople than one side of Edinburgh is unlike the other'.

Robert Chambers, a year earlier, had been in substantial agreement, remarking that 'the fine gentlemen, who daily exhibit their foreign dresses and manners in Princes Street, have no idea of the race of people who roost in the tall houses of the Lawnmarket, in the West Bow and in some of the sequestered closes and back courts of the Old Town'. He considered that 'there might be found specimens of people bearing nearly all the characteristics of 17th Century Edinburgh'.

There was truth in the criticism, but it was nevertheless essentially sentimental. The increase of wealth, the burgeoning of the middle class, was bound to lead to a degree of social stratification, as it did in London, Paris and, a hundred years later, Rome. To regret the days when a shop might occupy the ground floor of a house in the High Street, with a nobleman on

The High Street outside John Knox's House:
drawing by David Allan,
c. 1793

the floor above and a Writer to the Signet over his head, and then a tradesman's family or an artisan's, till one reached the most indigent in the garrets, is to wish that Edinburgh could have been held in a time-warp.

7

A City of Lawyers

It is impossible to exaggerate the importance of the legal
profession in Edinburgh's history; by the middle of the
eighteenth century it was truly a city of lawyers. Law was even
the hobby of shopkeepers and artisans, like Scott's Bartoline
Saddletree in *The Heart of Midlothian*. The reason for the
supremacy of the lawyers had been well expressed by a distinguished academic lawyer of our own day, Professor T. B. Smith:
'Scotland's supreme courts have sat on in Parliament House in
Edinburgh, symbolising, as it were, the nation's survival in her
laws.' Or as J. G. Lockhart, Scott's son-in-law and biographer,
put it, 'It is not to be denied that the Scottish lawyers have done
more than any other class to keep alive the sorely threatened
spirit of national independence in the thoughts and feelings of
their countrymen.' For this reason lawyers were accorded a
reverence in Edinburgh which they have seldom been granted, or
indeed deserved, elsewhere.

That the lawyers were able to assume this position was first
of all the result of the work of Lord Stair, Lord President of the
Court of Session after the revolution of 1688. Stair was an
unattractive man from a family with a sinister reputation. More
than anyone else he and his son, Sir John Dalrymple, Master of
Stair, were responsible for the iniquity of Glencoe. Stair himself
was said by his enemies to be in league with the devil (a
sufficiently familiar accusation in seventeenth-century Scotland;
his wife, with similar proclivities, was compared to the Witch of
Endor, and was said to have been observed sitting in the guise of
a cat on a cushion beside the Lord President). Their family life

*John Dalrymple, 2nd Earl of
Stair*
(anon.)

was understandably disturbed: one son died of poison; a daughter stabbed her bridegroom on their wedding night, this legend becoming the basis for Scott's most tragic novel, *The Bride of Lammermoor*; one grandson killed another. Nevertheless, Stair's reputation in legal circles could scarcely be higher, and he is known as the Father of Scots Law.

His great work was *The Institutes of the Law of Scotland*, published in 1681. This represents the most complete codification of Scots law and sets out its fundamental and enduring principles; it is the Old Testament of the profession, and it assumed an added importance in the absence of a Parliament in Edinburgh capable of creating new Statute Law. Scottish legal institutions were left free to develop without much legislative interference, or ministerial control, from London. The Senators of the Court of Session, acting with what was called 'native vigour', formed the habit of declaring what the law was, on the basis of precedent, natural law and the principles laid down by Stair. Michael Fry, in his biography of Henry Dundas, remarks that this habit 'gave the Scots judiciary something like the function which the Supreme Court of the United States enjoys today'.

The distinguishing feature of the system was that the College of Justice was precisely that: a college. Decisions were arrived at after debate between the judges. Sir Walter Scott, himself Clerk to the Court of Session for almost thirty years (as well as being Sheriff of Selkirkshire), might correctly observe that 'a court of 15 men, trained to polemical habits from their youth, is more fitted for the dexterities of a popular debate than for the gravity and decorum of judicial deliberation'. Cockburn's description of the Inner House in his youth might seem to support this view:

> It was so cased in venerable dirt that it was impossible to say whether it has ever been painted; but it was all of a dark brownish hue. There was a gallery over the bar, and so low that a barrister in a frenzy was in danger of hitting it. A huge fire-place stood behind the Lord President's chair, with one of the stone jambs cracked, and several bars of the large grate broken. That grate was at least half full of dust. It probably had never been cleaned since the institution of the Court in the sixteenth century.

In this 'dismal hole', justice was bickered over and dispersed, by judges who sat with their bottle of port or claret at their elbow from which they refreshed themselves the better to assess legal argument. One judge, Lord Newton, was said to be at his best only after he had imbibed six bottles of claret, perhaps three bottles of today's standard size. In his days as an advocate he was once visited by a client, who was surprised to be told that his lawyer was at dinner. 'I thought Mr Hay [as he then was] habitually dined at 5, and it is now but 4,' the client said. 'Aye,' replied the advocate's manservant, 'but he is at yesterday's dinner.'

Edinburgh was a convivial city, and the most learned judges might be equally celebrated for their prowess with a bottle as for their acumen in the law. This didn't prevent them dispensing justice with an authority that was rarely questioned.

There were remarkable men among them. There was Lord Kames, for example, judge, jurist, legal historian and philosopher, a Senator of the College for thirty years, till his death in 1782. He was that rare combination: a historian of the law who was also a bold reformer, having grasped that only someone with a deep understanding of the historical origins of a rule of law, and of its connections with particular social and economic conditions, can understand when it has outlived its utility and should be discarded. Like other eighteenth-century judges Kames spoke a rich, broad Scots and possessed a robust, sometimes brutal, humour. On one occasion, it was his duty to sentence a man with whom he had often played chess to death; he leant down from the bench and said, 'An' that's checkmate, Jamie.'

There was Lord Gardenstone, who was so fond of pigs that one slept in his bedroom on a bed prepared by his Lordship from the clothes he had removed and would wear the following morning, and there was Lord Monboddo, another philosopher, who believed that men had once had tails, but had lost them in the course of evolution, and that the orang-utan was an undeveloped human being, lacking only the gift of speech. Their eccentricities did not prevent either from being improving

landlords as well as learned judges, or Monboddo from making a valuable contribution to the understanding of how language had developed, even if he was to be disappointed with the orang-utan. There was Boswell's father, Lord Auchinleck, scornful of his son's infatuation with Dr Johnson, whom he dismissed as 'an auld dominie'. There was Lord Braxfield, the original of Stevenson's Weir of Hermiston, deeply learned in the dark recesses of feudal law, contemptuous of reformers and all those men without property who nevertheless claimed political rights, replying to one poor soul who protested that Jesus Christ was a reformer too, 'Muckle he made o' that, he was hangit.' 'You're a verrry clever chiel,' he told another, 'but you'd be nane the waur of a hanging.' And there were great legal families, Hopes, Erskines, Dundases, Homes, Dalrymples, Scotland's own *noblesse de la robe*, producing pleaders and judges, generation after generation, moulding the law, controlling Scottish society, dominating Edinburgh and revered by its citizens.

The Outer House of Parliament Hall was the place where advocates, Writers to the Signet and Solicitors to the Supreme Court mingled with their clients. It was a great empty space, except for the throng of people accustomed to discuss their business on the walk in order that their deliberations might be less easily overheard, a custom that still prevails today. Thence they might repair across the close to what Scott calls 'the Cimmerian abysses of John's Coffee-House' for their 'meridian', the noontime dram of brandy, rum or whisky, the drinking of which was an Edinburgh custom that ensured that coffee houses did a better trade in spirits than in tea or coffee.

For, if the lawyers, with some assistance from the ministers of the Kirk and the professors of the buoyant University, gave the city its intellectual tone, they also faithfully and enthusiastically shared in its convivial habits. Edinburgh was an intensely sociable place; it could scarcely be otherwise, for in the middle of the eighteenth century some 25,000 people were crammed into an area that you could walk end to end in a quarter of an hour, and across in little more than five minutes. It was a city of clubs and taverns, where men met to dispute, debate, feed and drink. Entertainment in the home was as rare as it still is in a

James Burnett, Lord Monboddo
by John Brown

Mediterranean city. The tavern was the meeting place, and most of the innumerable clubs held their session in public houses.

Chambers opens his chapter on Convivialia in his *Traditions of Edinburgh* as follows:

'The Parliament Close and Public Characters of Edinburgh, Fifty years since': style of John Kay

> Tavern dissipation, now so rare amongst the respectable classes of the community, formerly prevailed in Edinburgh to an incredible extent, and engrossed the leisure hours of all professional men, scarcely excepting even the most stern and dignified. No rank, class or profession, indeed, formed an exception to this rule. Nothing was so common in the morning as to meet men of high rank and official dignity reeling home from a close in the High Street where they had spent the night drinking. Nor was it unusual to find two or three of His Majesty's most honourable Lords of Council and Session mounting the bench in the forenoon in a crapulous state.

It could never be said that the judges of the great days of the Enlightenment lived at a rarefied remove from their fellow citizens. Eighteenth-century Edinburgh was, of necessity, an intimate city. The foreign observer who remarked that he could stand by the Mercat Cross and in half an hour take fifty men of genius by the hand might have added that they would all have known each other, and half a dozen as like as not would have supped together the previous evening. And this narrow society with, nevertheless, broad views took the tone of its speech and argument from the lawyers. The Faculty of Advocates was said to be 'the chief community of loungers and talkers in Edinburgh'. Even early in the nineteenth century Lockhart considered that 'the best table-talk of Edinburgh was, and probably still is, in a very great measure made up of brilliant disquisition – such as might be transformed without alteration to a professor's notebook, or the pages of a critical review – and of sharp word-catchings, ingenious thrusting and parrying of dialectics, and all the quips and Quibblets of bar pleading'.

Something of that tone survives to this day. You can hear its echo in the precision of old ladies in Morningside. Muriel Spark, brought up in Bruntsfield, educated at James Gillespie's School for Girls, has written that her 'whole education seemed to pivot' round the word 'nevertheless': 'All grades of society constructed sentences bridged by "nevertheless".' That is a legacy from the dominance of the lawyers in the Edinburgh of the Enlightenment.

Scotland was a nation distinct in itself and proud of its distinctiveness; nevertheless it was part of the United Kingdom of Great Britain, and within that kingdom the Faculty of Advocates and the Senators of the College of Justice nevertheless maintained the independence of Scotland. Their legal system might seem to have evolved in order to maintain the dominance of the class to which they belonged; nevertheless it was the proud possession of all Scotland. Had the independence of Scots law not been maintained at the union, it is hard to see how Scotland would have remained Scottish.

8

The Last Purely Scotch Age

Cockburn, nineteenth-century advocate, memorialist, architect of the Scottish Reform Bill, finally Lord Cockburn, Senator of the College of Justice, was given to melancholy. He lamented that the eighteenth century was 'the last purely Scotch age':

> Most of what had gone before had been turbulent and political. All that has come after has been English. The 18th was the final Scotch century. We, whose youth tasted the close of that century, and who have lived far into the Southern influence, feel proud of a purely Edinburgh society which raised the reputation of our discrowned capital, and graced the deathbed of the national manners. No wonder that we linger with affectionate respect over the deserted or degraded haunts of our distinguished people, and that we feel as if we could despise ourselves if we did not prefer the memory of those scenes to all that is to be found in the commonplace characters of modern men, and in the insignificance of modern refinement.

Cockburn was a man of both sense and sensibility, capable of relishing his mood whichever sentiment was for the moment uppermost. In robust form he considered that 'a wise man would like to have seen the past age, but to live in this one'. His instability accurately reflected the mood of many, then and subsequently. Old vanishing Edinburgh was to be mourned; we have already heard Cockburn groan (melodiously of course) over the building of the New Town – which he nevertheless inhabited.

Cockburn was born in 1779, when Edinburgh had already burst from its old confinement; Sir Walter Scott in 1771 in a house,

David Hume
by Louis Carrogis:
'the brightest star
in the firmament
of Edinburgh
intellectuals'

above
Dundas House, St Andrew Square
(Royal Bank of Scotland):
domed ceiling (banking hall)

above left
Allan Ramsay the Elder
by William Aikman

left
*Aerial view of the New Town
from the east*

right
Robert Adam attributed
to George Willison, c. 1770–75

Lord Braxfield by Sir Henry Raeburn

The High Street (c. 1793) by David Allan

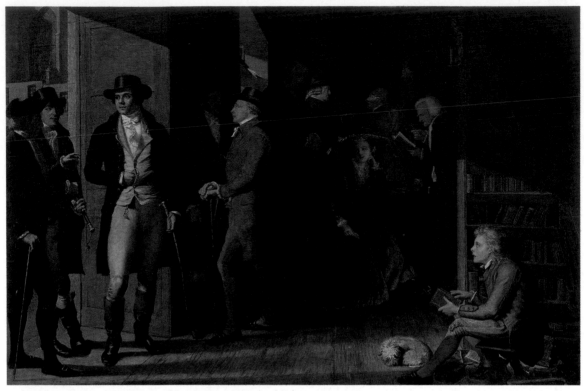

Robert Burns in James Sibbald's Circulating Library, Parliament Square
by William Borthwick Johnstone. The young Walter Scott is seated in the foreground

Edinburgh from Arthur's Seat by Hugh Williams, c. 1826. A luminous image of Scott's 'own romantic town'

Sir Walter Scott by Sir Henry Raeburn, 1822

Edinburgh from Canonmills attributed to John Knox, c. 1820–25

The Entry of George IV into Edinburgh from the Calton Hill, 1822 by John Wilson Ewbank

Lord Cockburn: marble bust by
William Brodie, 1855

long since demolished, in College Wynd. Their lifetimes spanned
Edinburgh's period of greatest glory, already fading when Scott
died in 1832. Night, Cockburn might have said, had succeeded
twilight before he himself passed away in 1847. Scott's monument still dominates Princes Street, while Cockburn has given his
name to the association that seeks to preserve the city from
spoliation.

In the years between their births came the death of a man
whose brief life and vigorous work seem to justify Cockburn's

plaint: the poet Robert Fergusson (1750–74). Born in Cap-and-Feather Close, soon to disappear as a result of the building of the North Bridge, Fergusson, son of a clerk who had come to the city from Aberdeenshire, was educated at the High School at the eastern end of the Cowgate. He attended St Andrews University, and then became a clerk in the Commissary Office in Edinburgh.

Robert Fergusson by Alexander Runciman

The work was undemanding, and he entered, as enthusiastic as any student, wit or poet, into the joys of tavern life, soon being elected to membership of the Cape Club, which met over oysters,

opposite
Tavern interior
('The Jolly Beggars')
by Alexander Carse

rizzar'd haddock (fish dried in the sun and wind) and gin at James Mann's tavern in Craig's Close. His poetry, all written in the three years between his return to the city and his wretched death, probably from *delirium tremens*, in the asylum, gives the most vivid picture of the social life of the day. It is written in a vigorous and natural Scots:

> When big as burns the gutters rin,
> Gin ye hae catcht a droukit skin,
> To Luckie Middlemist's loup in,
>   And sit fu snug
> O'er oysters and a dram o' gin
>   Or haddock lug.

> When auld Saunt Giles, at aught o'clock,
> Gars merchant lowns their chopies lock,
> There we adjourn wi' hearty fowk
>   To birle our bodles,
> And get wharewi' to crack our joke
>   And clear our noddles.

There is an irresistible zest to his picture of tavern life, but poor Fergusson was not blind to the darker side of things:

> Near some lamp-post wi' dowy face,
> Wi' heavy een, and sour grimace,
> Stands she that beauty lang had kend,
> Whoredom her trade, and vice her end.
> But see whare now she wuns her bread,
> By that which nature ne'er decreed;
> And sings sad music to the lugs,
> 'many burachs o' damn'd whores and rogues.

Fergusson should be read in bulk; he is not one of those poets who yield their best to the anthologist. In this, as perhaps in his manner also, he resembles Byron more than Burns. Burns, however, admired him greatly, and learned from him:

> Oh thou my elder brother in Misfortune,
> By far my elder brother in the Muse,
> With tears I pity thy unhappy fate!
> Why is the Bard unfitted for the world,
> Yet has so keen a relish of its pleasures?

Burns, partly because he made his first visit to Edinburgh in 1786 when he was already a celebrity and his character formed, partly because he had a greater sense of his own dignity and worth, never experienced misfortune on the same scale as Fergusson. Burns was not wholly at his ease in Edinburgh, caught between his natural inclinations and the demands of polite society, between his democratic instincts and the need to flatter those who could make his way easier; but the young Walter Scott, who met him in the house of the philosopher Adam Ferguson (part of the house, then called Sciennes Hill, still remains in Braid Place), observed that 'I never saw such an eye in a human head, though I have seen most of the distinguished men of my time'. He found him, in that gathering more notable for learning than for rank, perfectly self-confident: 'He expressed himself with perfect firmness, but without the least intrusive forwardness.'

Scott belongs to Edinburgh as Burns didn't, though he also belongs, with an even more deep-rooted affection, to the Borders. The record of his moves in the city follows the course of its development away from its medieval past. His birthplace in College Wynd was a high tenement in a stinking alley where the houses were so close together that a man could reach across from his window and shake the hand of the occupant of the house opposite. The neighbourhood was unhealthy, and six of Scott's brothers and sisters died in infancy; he himself contracted polio (which left him with a limp) and was lucky to survive. His father's prospering law business permitted a removal to the healthier locality of George Square (no. 25), where their neighbours included the Lord Advocate, Henry Dundas (who lodged with his mother there), Lord Braxfield, and Jean, Duchess of Gordon.

It was in that house that two incidents occurred which made a deep impression on the young boy, for both seemed to fan the dying embers of the Jacobite romance. At that time, as Scott was to recall in the introduction to *Redgauntlet*, there were still many to be met in Edinburgh who had been 'as the established phrase gently worded it, out in the Forty-Five. . . . Jacobites were looked on in society as men who had proved their sincerity by sacrificing their interests to their principles; and in well-regulated companies, it was held a piece of ill-breeding to injure their feelings or ridicule the compromises by which they endeavoured to keep themselves abreast of the current of the day.'

His first encounter was with a Highland gentleman, Alexander Stewart of Invernahyle, who possessed an added glamour for the boy because he had once crossed swords with Rob Roy Macgregor himself. Greatly daring, Scott asked him if he had ever been afraid. The hero replied that in his first battle he was so afraid that he would have given any man a hundred marks to assure him he would not run away. Scott never forgot this; the heroes of the Waverley novels walk a narrow line, not only between rival causes and fanaticisms, but between fear and fortitude, self-interest and self-regard.

The other meeting was a reminder of how old animosities die hard. His father had some clients who preferred to visit him at his own house under cover of darkness. One such, Scott remembered, sent a servant boy down into the street to see that it was deserted before he dared take his leave. When he did so, Scott's father hurled the glass from which his client had been drinking into the fireplace. 'No member of my household,' he said, 'shall drink from a glass that has touched the lips of Mr Murray of Broughton', for his mysterious visitor had been none other than that dishonoured man who had been the prince's secretary and then saved his own skin by bearing witness against his fellow Jacobites. With such childhood memories it was no wonder Scott became the novelist he did.

His lameness denied him his preferred career as a soldier. So he was apprenticed to his father, and slaved in his office copying legal documents: 'drudgery', he called it. Then he was called to the Bar, a sign that the family was rising in the world, since the status of advocate was more distinguished than that even of a Writer to the Signet like his father. He made no great career there, and was happy to be appointed to the two posts of Clerk to the Court of Session and Sheriff of Selkirkshire. He performed his duties diligently in both positions, but his heart was not in the law, though his experience provided good copy for his novels. His true life was in his imagination and in his beloved Borders. He enjoyed Edinburgh, but it was a place for labour rather than pleasure.

He never felt any great warmth for the house in North Castle Street to which he removed after his marriage in 1797. He left it with only mild regret when it had to be sold after his financial disaster in 1826, even though he confessed that he was 'subject to attachment even to tables and chairs'. But it would have broken his heart if he had been compelled to leave Abbotsford, the house he had built by the Tweed.

His last Edinburgh years were spent in lodgings: first in St David Street, in what a friend described as 'lowly squalor', then in Walker Street and finally in Shandwick Place, though he would sometimes stay with his publisher Robert Cadell in Atholl Crescent. These last three lodgings were all to the west of the

George Square, west side. Scott's house (No. 25) is in the centre

original New Town, beyond Charlotte Square. This new West
End was still under construction. Returning to his lodging one
night, Scott tumbled into a builders' trench.

Scott's cast of mind was historical. His great Edinburgh novel, *The
Heart of Midlothian*, is set a generation before his own birth. He called
Edinburgh 'mine own Romantic town' and, being sociable, took
pleasure in its varied and vigorous society, but he was more easily
moved by past glories than by the evidence of progress which the
present afforded. Cockburn resembled him in his passionate
attachment to a disappearing Scotland, which feeling, coming close
to sentimentality at times, was nevertheless coupled with a
common-sense acceptance that, to use one of Scott's favourite
Shakespeare quotations, 'Things must be as they may.'

The two differed in politics, however; this was a sign of the
changing temper of Edinburgh and Scotland. In the previous
generation, once the Jacobite cause was dead, political strife had
been rare. There was a consensus that the Scottish interest could
best be served by excluding political questions from general
discussion; indeed some of the learned societies actually forbade
political debate. It could be argued that, far from being a
limitation, this allowed more fruitful discussion, free from party
bias. In any case it was generally felt that Scotsmen had a
common interest in view of the country's subsidiary position in
the union.

The consensus evaporated in the 1790s, when Scott was a
young man and Cockburn still a boy. The cause was the
revolution in France, for this divided society between those who
generally approved the revolution's assertion of the Rights of
Man and its questioning of the established order, and those who
thought that such inquiry, by bringing ancient principles and
modes of life under scrutiny, and thus exposing them to adverse
criticism, threatened the fundamental stability of society. The
debate was acute in Edinburgh, because the whole tendency of
the philosophical historians of the Scottish Enlightenment, and
their elaboration of 'the Scottish Science of Man', should have
been sympathetic to French ideas. After all, as the country grew
richer, and as these riches were more widely diffused, it was not

logical that the right to political representation should be frozen and confined to those who had acquired that right at an earlier stage in the progress of society. However that might be, the revolution in France alarmed the propertied classes in Scotland, and the alarm was as keenly felt in philosophical Edinburgh as anywhere.

The outcome was a period of repression. The Societies of the Friends of the People were outlawed, and their leaders put on trial for sedition. The trial of the most prominent, a lawyer and laird called Thomas Muir of Huntershill, was conducted by Braxfield. The Crown's case was entrusted to the Lord Advocate's nephew, Robert Dundas, who described the accused as 'a demon of mischief . . . tainted from head to foot, and as unworthy to live under the protection of the law as the meanest felon'. Braxfield found no difficulty in agreeing. He had picked a jury composed of known government supporters. He told them that reform was intrinsically unconstitutional. It followed that to seek it was seditious. Only the landed interest, said the old feudal lawyer, had the right to be represented in Parliament. 'As for the rabble who have nothing but personal property, what hold has the nation on them? What security for the payment of their taxes? They may pack up their property on their backs and leave the country in the twinkling of an eye. But landed property cannot be removed.' He assured the jury that the French were 'monsters of human nature', and sentenced Muir to transportation for fourteen years.

The glee with which Braxfield meted out sentence disgusted even some of those who agreed with him. Cockburn thought his conduct disgraceful, called him 'the Jeffreys of Scotland', yet could not conceal a sneaking regard, occasioned by his rough humour and mastery of demotic Scots. All the same, Lord Advocate Dundas deemed it wiser not to employ him in later trials. There should, it was thought, be a decency in everything, even in sentencing seditious persons.

The danger of revolution was slight, probably did not exist. Nevertheless Dundas took precautions. He had the Act against Wrongeous Imprisonment – Scotland's *habeas corpus* – suspended. He employed a network of spies to penetrate any possibly dissident groups, also to provoke words and actions which could expose them to the rigour of the law. Cockburn thought there was a general witch-hunt against political dissent. He may have been right. He reckoned that the French Revolution, and the fear it occasioned, dominated the years of his youth.

There was genuine fear of invasion. Volunteer forces were raised to resist the French, though the only action they saw was directed against poor rioters, often seeking nothing but bread. Scott served in the Royal Edinburgh Light Dragoons; Cockburn commanded a company of the First Royal Edinburgh Volunteers. Eleven people were killed at Tranent when rioting over the Militia Act was suppressed.

Respectable men recoiled from the excesses of the revolution, seeing the French as murdering fanatics. Yet the old order was coming in for renewed criticism. Soon the Whigs saw parliamentary reform as a means of averting the danger of revolution by enlarging the electorate to include the prosperous and educated. They did not want democracy, but nevertheless it seemed absurd that the electorate of Scotland should number fewer than 4000 people. It was grotesque that Edinburgh's representation in Parliament should be controlled by the Town Council, a corrupt and self-electing oligarchy, in thrall to the Lord Advocate Dundas, numbering thirty-three persons and described by Cockburn as 'silent, powerful, submissive, mysterious and impenetrable, they might have been sitting in Venice'.

There was no chance of reform in the 1790s; the mood generated by the war with France was against it, for it was easy to tar any reformer with the French brush. Moreover Dundas continued to exercise a benign yet repressive authority over all public appointments, and even over the public expression of opinion. Yet things were changing.

Cockburn attributed his intellectual awakening to his membership of two societies: the Academical, formed in 1796 and lasting till 1816, and the Speculative, dating from 1799. 'My reason no sooner began to open,' he wrote in his *Memorials*, 'and to get some fair play, than the distressing wisdom of my ancestors began to fade, and the more attractive sense that I met with among the young men into whose company our debating societies threw me, gradually hardened me into what I became – whatever this was.' What it was, in political terms, was a New Whig. So were his friends, Francis Jeffrey, Henry Brougham and Francis Horner. They were all lawyers – Jeffrey would in time be Lord Advocate (with Cockburn as Solicitor-General), and Brougham Lord Chancellor, all in the Whig government that put through the Reform Bills of 1832; but they were not confined to the narrow interests of their profession.

In 1802, along with an English clergyman resident in Edinburgh, the famous wit Sydney Smith, they founded a magazine, the *Edinburgh Review*. The publisher was the Napoleonic Archibald Constable (Scott's publisher also). Scott called him 'the prince of booksellers', and Cockburn thought that 'the literature of Scotland has been more indebted [to Constable] than to any other of his vocation'. It was thanks to Constable, and those who were inspired by his example, that Edinburgh became the greatest publishing centre in Britain in the early nineteenth century, a distinction it did not relinquish till well on in Victoria's reign. Constable's shop was in Princes Street, across the road from where the North British Hotel now stands. Cockburn attributed Constable's success to his realisation that authors deserved to be well paid:

> Abandoning the old timid and grudging system, Constable stood out as the general patron of all promising publications, and confounded not merely his rivals in trade, but his very authors, by his unheard-of prices. Ten, even twenty, guineas for a sheet of a review, £2,000 or £3,000 for a single poem, and £1,000 for two philosophical dissertations, drew authors from dens where they would otherwise have starved, and made Edinburgh a literary mart, famous with strangers, and the pride of its own citizens.

overleaf
Archibald Constable
by Andrew Geddes, 1813

Lord Francis Jeffrey
by William Bewick

Jeffrey edited the *Edinburgh Review* from his home in Buccleuch Place, just behind George Square. Its politics were Whig, and therefore it placed itself in opposition to the government of the day, still dominated by Dundas, who had now been created Lord Melville. The first edition of 750 copies sold out almost at once, and it was soon exercising an influence on taste and opinion far

beyond its circulation. That, however, rose steadily: 7,000 within five years, and monthly sales of over 14,000 were reached by the mid-1820s.

Whatever its influence on political opinion, in literary matters Jeffrey's taste was as timid as the expression of his opinions was savage. He could see no merit in the English Lake Poets, considering that Wordsworth's long poem *The Excursion* 'would never do'. The *Review*'s attack on Byron's first collection provoked his satire, *English Bards and Scotch Reviewers*. He excelled himself in his attack on Scott's *Marmion*:

> To write a modern romance of chivalry seems to be such a
> phantasy as to build a modern abbey or an English
> pagoda. For once, however, it may be excused as a pretty
> caprice of genius; but a second production of the same
> sort is entitled to less indulgence, and imposes a sort of
> duty to drive the author from so idle a task, by a fair
> exposition of the faults which are, in a manner,
> inseparable from its expression.

The choice of the word 'faults' reveals Jeffrey's lack of understanding of the Romantic sensibility. His preference was for artificial diction and deliberate design, the outmoded 'correctness' of the eighteenth century. He encouraged his readers 'to adopt a style of literary and political principles, which was rooted, not in eternal principles, but in the ordinary experience of ordinary literate and responsible men living in a modern age'. In Carlyle's opinion Jeffrey's influence was baleful:

> Democracy, the gradual uprise and rule in all things of
> roaring, million-headed, unreflecting, darkly suffering,
> darkly sinning Demos come to call old superiors to
> account, at its maddest of tribunals: nothing in my time
> has so forwarded this as Jeffrey and his once-famous
> *Edinburgh Review*.

Certainly, whatever Carlyle's exaggerations, Jeffrey's combination of artistic timidity and liberal political views prepared the way for the domination of thought by conventional bourgeois respectability, characteristic of the nineteenth century.

Carlyle's criticism of Jeffrey went beyond the personal. His recognition of Jeffrey's failure was at the same time a criticism and recognition of the weakness and loss of vitality in Scottish culture. Jeffrey, Carlyle thought, reduced criticism to a level of banality. Yet he also found that in conversation Jeffrey evinced finer talents than he displayed in writing, especially when he spoke Scots. 'Here,' he wrote, 'is a man whom they have kneaded into the shape of an Edinburgh Reviewer, and clothed the soul of in Whig formulas . . . but he might have been a beautiful Goldoni, too, or something better in that kind, and given us beautiful comedies, and aerial pictures, true and poetic, of Human Life, in a far other way.' Or he was 'a potential Voltaire'; but, as it was, 'he was not deep enough, pious or reverent enough to have been great in Literature'. The charge, personal as it is, has a wider application: the *Edinburgh Review* achieved a remarkable authority, but it diluted the distinctiveness of Scottish culture; and in Jeffrey's unwillingness to come to serious engagement with the best work of his own time represented a retreat from the pioneering audacity of the great age of the Enlightenment.

The *Edinburgh Review* spawned imitators and rivals. The most vigorous of these was *Blackwood's*, founded in 1817, by the already prosperous bookseller and publisher William Blackwood, the Scottish agent for Byron's publisher, John Murray. The previous year Blackwood had moved his business from South Bridge to 17 Princes Street, where he founded what one of the contributors to his *Maga*, Scott's son-in-law, John Gibson Lockhart, called 'the only great lounging book-shop in the New Town'. Lockhart remarks that 'the prejudice in favour of sticking by the Old Town was so strong among gentlemen of the trade that when the bookseller intimated his purpose of removing to the New, his ruin was immediately prophesied by not a few of his sagacious brethren.' He defied their doubts, to good effect.

His magazine was intended from the first to be a Tory competitor for the *Edinburgh Review*. It began badly, and Blackwood soon got rid of the editors he had appointed, replacing them with Lockhart and John Wilson, two young men distinguished for their sense of their own superiority, their intolerance, their high spirits and combative natures. Wilson, the

son of a Paisley manufacturer, a graduate (like Lockhart) of Oxford, was an admirer and undistinguished imitator of the Lake Poets. They recruited James Hogg, the Ettrick Shepherd, a remarkable self-educated mixture of genius and gaucherie, and took the town by storm with the *Chaldee Manuscript*, a satirical picture, written in the language of the Old Testament, of the leading political and literary figures of the day, the Whigs being attacked with considerable scurrility and the Tories praised for their intelligence. A Highland lady, Mrs Grant of Laggan, reported that the city was 'in an uproar about *Blackwood's Magazine*, which contains in a very irreverent and unjustifiable form, a good deal of wit and cunning satire'.

The centrepiece of the magazine soon became the *Noctes Ambrosianae*, conversations between the principal contributors reputedly taking place in Ambrose's Tavern in Picardy Place. No doubt they were to some extent versions of real conversations; no doubt various writers contributed bits to them, and rewrote what others had sketched; but they soon became principally the work of Wilson, though the main figure in the dialogues was usually a caricatured version of Hogg. They are hard to read now, and much of the wit has faded or seems forced and mechanical, but as a device for offering free-ranging commentary on the political, social and literary affairs of the day, the form was admirable. The *Noctes* were vigorous, pungent, intellectual and challenging.

Lockhart departed to London to edit the *Quarterly*; Hogg spent most of his last years farming, not successfully, in his native Borders; Wilson, the least of the three, was left in charge. He became, by reason of the force of his personality, a great Edinburgh figure, striding huge and bare-headed along Princes Street, half a dozen terriers at his heels. In 1820, as the result of a political ramp, he was appointed Professor of Moral Philosophy at the University, though it was generally agreed that he knew no philosophy, and his lectures were written for him by a friend, Alexander Blair, who lived in Birmingham. Addicted to whisky punch, as timid and conventional in his judgements as he was bold and flamboyant in expression, envious of other Blackwood's writers (Hogg and Galt) whom he rightly suspected to have a greater genius than himself, Wilson is, with Jeffrey, the most

William Blackwood by Sir William Allan, 1830

characteristic figure of this period when the flames of the Enlightenment were dying down. Carlyle, with that peculiar acuteness which he brought to his judgement of others, thought him to have the makings of a great man; 'yet the great man never was, nor perhaps ever could be, quite made'.

Professor John Wilson ('Christopher North') by Thomas Duncan

There were other signs that Edinburgh could no longer be all-sufficient in the old manner. Francis Horner, one of the co-founders of the *Edinburgh Review*, took off for London complaining that 'to one resident in the stagnation or poverty of Edinburgh conversation, the *beaux-esprits* of London are entertaining and instructive novelties'. He added that 'I become daily more averse to the practice of the Scots Courts.' This was the time when young Whig lawyers found it hard to get briefs, which may explain why reasons for emigrating 'occurred daily to his meditation'. Boswell, a couple of generations earlier, had preferred the irresponsibility of London to the narrower confines and domesticity of Edinburgh; but Horner was a serious man in a way that Boswell was not. The truth was that Edinburgh was already in danger of sinking into provinciality.

The fiasco of the National Monument spoke of a loss of confidence, even though this might be contradicted by the ambitious work of architects like William Playfair and Thomas Hamilton. The monument, intended as Edinburgh's Parthenon, was to be erected in honour of Britain's victory over Napoleon. A public subscription raised £24,000 and it was hoped that parliament would pay the balance. It did not, so the monument was never completed. The comment in the *Noctes* was apt: 'We admire the Parthenon. We resolve to build it. We call ourselves Athenians, and then implore parliament to pay the piper. Poor devils! we ought to be ashamed of ourselves.' Already a tune about abandoned schemes, with which modern Edinburgh and modern Scotland have now become familiar, was being piped.

The half-finished monument still stands on Calton Hill, more agreeable perhaps in its apparently ruinous state than if it had been completed. Its companion, the Nelson Monument, was of course completed, but, as James Grant remarked in *Old and New Edinburgh* (1888), there were many who would have wished it had suffered the same fate as the imitation of the Parthenon.

He thought it 'an edifice in such doubtful taste that its demolition has been more than once advocated', yet he admitted that 'with all its defects it makes a magnificent termination to the vista along Princes Street'. As for what was meant to be 'a literal restoration of the Parthenon at Athens':

> . . . notwithstanding the enthusiasm displayed when the undertaking was originated, and though a vast amount of money was subscribed, the former subsided, and the

western peristyle alone was partially erected. In consequence of this remarkable end to an enterprise that was begun under the most favourable auspices, the national monument is often referred to as 'Scotland's pride and poverty'. The pillars are of gigantic proportions, formed of beautiful Craigleith stone; each block weighed from ten to fifteen tons, and each column as it stands, with the base and frieze, cost upward of £1,000. As a ruin it gives a classic aspect to the whole city. According to the original idea part of this edifice was to be used as a Scottish Valhalla.

The National Monument,
Calton Hill

The Calton Hill had been opened up by the building of Waterloo Place, which had required the enormous expense of bridging Laigh Wynd. Fortunately the Regent Road was built on the cheap, the labour being provided by those on poor relief. One consequence of this construction of a new and dignified entrance to Edinburgh from the south-east was the acceleration of the decay of the Canongate, the old entry to the city. By 1833 it was said that only one 'person of quality' lived there. The author of an article in the *Edinburgh Review*, probably Jeffrey himself, hoped that the imitation Parthenon would not only serve as a model for future building, so that within twenty years 'no architect, not even a stone mason will repeat, even in Gothic architecture, such things as we see everywhere risen, and, we fear, still rising about us', but also instil a sense of the sublime in the national soul.

Yet there is one curious circumstance. For all the talk about it being Scotland's disgrace, and for all the windy eloquence that promised 'a Westminster Abbey for Scotland' (Cockburn's phrase), it may never have been seriously intended to be more than a folly, a picturesque false ruin. The architectural critic and historian Charles McKean states that 'what was built was exactly what the contract drawings specified *should* be built. In other words, it was a deliberate intention from the first to build only the small section that we can see.' The evidence of the drawings is convincing, but, if this was the intention, the secret was well kept; the result an example of Edinburgh's taste for duality.

Another ruin spectacularly enlivened the Edinburgh scene in 1822. This was His Majesty King George IV. George, lachrymose, artistic, selfish and spendthrift, was the most engaging but unpopular member of his generally charmless family. His unpopularity in London had sunk to new depths in the year after his accession in 1820, principally because of his attempt to divorce his sluttish wife, Caroline of Brunswick. The London mob took up her cause; Brougham defended her; the king was humiliated.

His journey north was therefore a sort of escape. It was seized upon by his ministers as a useful political demonstration. There had been recent outbreaks of Radical rioting in the Lowlands, even in Edinburgh; the king's presence might lend

some support to the established order. Scott, whose company
and novels the king enjoyed, and whom he had created baronet
in 1818, acted as Master of Ceremonies. He saw it as an
opportunity to reconcile all Scotland to royalty, and the
Highlands to the Lowlands. Accordingly, in the words of one of
George's biographers, Shane Leslie, 'Holyrood was turned into a
Waverley novel', though the king did not in fact stay there,
preferring the greater comfort of the Duke of Buccleuch's palace
at Dalkeith. Nevertheless he spent an hour at Holyrood exploring
the long deserted quarters of Mary, Queen of Scots. George had
the Romantic sensibility; he chose to be alone on this occasion.

   He paraded along Princes Street dressed in the kilt, with
flesh-coloured tights shielding the royal limbs from Edinburgh's
perpetual wind. The Highlanders whom Scott had marshalled
made a splendid show. Edinburgh, somewhat self-consciously,
blossomed. The event, whatever its inherent absurdities, served

*Incident during the visit of
George IV to Edinburgh, 1822:*
drawing by Sir David Wilkie.
Group includes two figures
in Highland dress and one in
the uniform of the Royal
Company of Archers (the
royal bodyguard)

the purpose Scott had designed. It was like the final chorus of an opera: Highlands and Lowlands, Jacobite and Whig, Scotland and England, joined together to sing the praise of the fat and florid king.

For all his faults, George played his part perfectly. He loved being on show, and he had the intelligence and sensibility to understand the significance of his performance. He acted with the same sensitivity and sense of what was fitting as he had manifested in the commission he had given to the great sculptor Canova to raise a monument to the exiled Jacobite kings in St Peter's in Rome.

The visit was significant in two ways. First, it pointed the direction that the monarchy would have to take if it was to survive in what would soon be the age of bourgeois Parliamentary democracy. The monarch was to be the figurehead, the focus of national loyalty, the symbol of national unity. George was fully conscious of what he was doing; at the same time sufficient of a natural actor to relish the part.

Second, it indicated Edinburgh's future role, its new industry indeed. No longer in any true sense a national capital, bereft of political importance greater than that of any other provincial city, having less indeed than Glasgow, Manchester and Birmingham would achieve in the nineteenth century, no longer the city of the Enlightenment which could give lessons to all Europe, the Athens of the North was well on the way to becoming what the Athens of the South already was: a city given over to the picturesque. Its future was as a centre of Romantic tourism.

Edinburgh had become a city in love with its own past.

9

The Underside of Things

There was, of course, an underside to Edinburgh, as to all cities. The early years of the nineteenth century were turbulent. Fear of the French kept the authorities alive to the dangers of sedition. Radicalism in any form was feared; in 1808, in a civil case brought against some paper-makers in Edinburgh, the Court of Session declared 'combination' (the forming of a trade union) to be an offence at Common Law. Lord Meadowbank rested his judgement on the principle that 'a measure of this kind destroys the freedom of the market'. That freedom was soon to cause much hardship. The ending of the war against Napoleon brought about an industrial depression. Demand dropped; discharged soldiers were looking for jobs; unemployment was high. In 1817 there were 1,600 workmen registered as unemployed by the Town Council and engaged, for subsistence wages, to build the roads round the Calton Hill and the Salisbury Crags. There were many more who were not registered, and who supported themselves by begging or crime.

The town was unruly, all the more so as social segregation developed, and the population grew rapidly. In 1811 it was just over 100,000; ten years later it had risen to 138,235. Immigrants came not only from the Lothians, Fife and the Borders, but from the Highlands, where the glens were being cleared for sheep, and from Ireland. They were crammed into the decaying tenements of the Old Town and its closes. A police force had been created in 1805 to replace the old and incompetent City Guard, but it had a hard job maintaining order.

In 1812 there were meal riots, and more than six hundred people were charged as beggars under the Vagrancy Act. The celebration of Hogmanay at the Iron Kirk that year turned into something more than the permissible exuberance of the season.

A Beggar with a Donkey
by David Allan

Towards midnight the High Street and Lawnmarket were taken over by gangs of youths armed with sticks or shillelaghs. They attacked the police, and knocked down and robbed respectable citizens whom they relieved of money, watches and hats. Three boys, all under the age of eighteen, were arrested and tried in March for their part in the affray. All were hanged in April, and all three scapegoats had Highland names: MacDonald, MacIntosh and Sutherland.

The most alarming riot took place in 1818, and nothing more surely displays the fragility of the social order than this outbreak, sparked off by the botched execution of a convicted thief, Robert Johnstone. It was a shocking affair, which provoked severe criticism of the magistrates and police. One observer, a student called William Macbean, described it in a letter to his mother as 'a second outbreak of the Porteous mob'.

It was initially the fault of the hangman, who miscalculated the drop. The wretched Johnstone was suspended, being slowly strangled, with his toes still touching the table. The crowd, already sympathetic to him, grew restive. Someone called out that the man's feet were still on the scaffold. The platform was rushed, and the magistrates prudently retired into St Giles, while the police attempted to recover their prisoner.

The scene was later described by a spectator in a letter to *The Scotsman* published over the name of *Civis Edinesis*:

> A spectacle now presented itself which equalled in horror anything ever witnessed in Paris during the Revolution. The unhappy Johnstone, half-alive, stript of parts of his clothes, so that the whole of his naked back was exhibited, lay extended on the ground, in front of the police office. At last some of the police officers, laying hold of the unhappy man, dragged him trailing along the ground, for about twenty paces into their den, which is also in the old Cathedral.

There he was revived, while a magistrate summoned a detachment of the 88th Foot (or Connaught Rangers) from the castle, and the hanging was resumed.

'The butchery,' *Civis Edinesis* complained, 'continued until twenty-three minutes past four o'clock, long after the street lamps were lighted for the night, and the moon and stars clearly visible.'

Naturally there was criticism of the magistrates, who naturally declared themselves fully satisfied with their own performance and paid the police chief, Captain Brown, an honorarium of £100 for 'his great exertions at the execution', though *Civis Edinesis* denied that he had performed any such, alleging instead that he had remained 'sitting in his own room . . . and though he had a reserve of between eighty and ninety of the best policemen in the Court Room, he remained inactive for between twenty and twenty-five minutes, and never ventured to show his face till he was sure the military were on the ground.'

Perhaps Captain Brown also had a lively memory of what had happened to Captain Porteous.

This riot was a good indication of the uncertain temper of the people from the lower parts of the town. The contrast between New and Old Town struck many. It was now that an American visitor, Nathaniel Willis, thought that 'Paris is not more unlike Constantinople than one side of Edinburgh is unlike the other'. It was not only foreigners who were so struck. In 1833 Robert Chambers wrote:

> The fine gentlemen, who daily exhibit their foreign dresses and manners on Princes Street, have no idea of the race of people who roost in the tall houses of the Lawnmarket and in the West Bow. In some of the sequestered closes of the Old Town, there may at this very day be found specimens of people bearing nearly all the characteristics of seventeenth century Edinburgh.

Some of them were 'creatures of inconceivable hideousness and surpassing horror'.

Two such had become infamous in the winter of 1828-9. Burke and Hare, names forever joined together, were Irish immigrants who had been originally drawn to Edinburgh by the prospect of work digging the Union Canal. They settled in the city, in more agreeable occupations, Hare working as a shoe-maker and Burke keeping a lodging house in the West Port. Then they saw an opportunity of enriching themselves by supplying bodies to the medical schools.

There was a ready market, for the study of anatomy was developing fast and the reputation of Edinburgh as the place to study medicine was already established. It was true that the

Professor of Anatomy, Alexander Munro, was not much good –
he had inherited the post formerly held by both his father and his
grandfather, whose lecture notes he was reputed to read to his
students. But there was a rival – the conservator at the Royal
College of Surgeons, Dr Robert Knox. He was a go-ahead man, at
the forefront of his profession, and he attracted the most eager
students.

The supply of bodies was, however, strictly regulated and
Knox found it insufficient for his needs. His assistant, one
Patterson, undertook to secure more corpses. He found Burke
and Hare, whom he had met in a tavern, sympathetic to his
difficulties, and they contracted to supply the deficiency: there
were, after all, graves to be robbed, while some poor people
might be persuaded, for a consideration, to hand over the bodies
of their dear departed. That was how it began, but Burke and
Hare soon found that the business could be more profitably and
comfortably managed if they cut out such middlemen and saw to
the provision of bodies themselves. Burke's lodging house gave
them a suitable workshop, and so they embarked on murder as a
commercial enterprise, in keeping, it may be said, with the new
spirit of the age. Over the period of a few months they supplied
Knox's students with at least sixteen bodies.

Success went to their heads. They grew careless in the
selection of their victims. Investigations followed and the pair
were arrested. Hare turned King's Evidence, without which,
legal opinion had it, conviction would have been impossible.
Burke admitted to some murders in a successful attempt to
persuade the jury to bring in a verdict of 'Not Proven' against his
mistress, Helen MacDougall, who had been associated with him
in the charge. Cockburn, her counsel, had some justification for
observing that 'Burke, except that he murdered, was a gentle-
manly fellow'.

Burke's execution on 28 January 1829, at the head of
Liberton's Wynd, was a hugely popular occasion. In *Blackwood's
Magazine*, Wilson ('Christopher North') thoroughly approved the
crowd's sentiments, which a journalist in the *Courant* had
deplored. The crowd yelled for Knox and Hare, but were not
satisfied. Later Burke's body was itself anatomised by Dr Munro,

The Execution of William Burke:
contemporary engraving (anon.)

and more than 20,000 people turned up to see it, some buying snuff boxes made from his skin. In April, Patterson wrote to Sir Walter Scott, suggesting that he should write on the subject of Burke and Hare and offering him his 'invaluable collection of anecdotes'. Scott was indignant, and called him 'Knox's jackal for buying murdered bodies'. Knox himself had already been examined by 'an independent and influential committee' which reported on 13 March 1829 that there was no evidence showing that he or his assistants knew that murder had been committed, but that he should perhaps have exercised 'more care in the reception of the bodies at the Anatomical class-rooms'. 'Christopher North' did not agree: 'How, in the nature of things, could Burke and Hare have been believed endowed with an instinct that led them to sixteen different houses in eight months, where the inmates were ready to sell their dead to the doctors?' He was equally offended to hear that Knox's students had received him with cheers when he returned to the lecture room. The truth surely is that Knox preferred to ask no questions; we have seen more than enough of that sort of behaviour in our own century.

For those more sensitive than Wilson, the whole episode was disturbing. Scott reflected that the progress of civilisation had left many behind, 'brutalised and degraded', and that 'the same nation at the same time displays the very highest and very lowest state in which the human race can exist in point of intellect'. At the same time, Knox had shown a moral infirmity. He offered 'a horrid example of how men may stumble and fall in the full match of intellect'.

Blackfriars' Wynd
by James Drummond, 1857

The gulf between rich and poor was not, however, a matter only of morality or intellect. An outbreak of cholera in 1832 devastated the overcrowded and insanitary dwellings of the Old Town. Twenty years later Dr George Bell published a pamphlet in which he denounced living conditions there. He found that 159 closes lacked drainage and a fresh water supply. In Blackfriars Wynd he counted 142 dwellings housing more than a thousand people. Most of these dwellings consisted of a single room, with five or six occupants. The evangelical minister Thomas Guthrie, who would later found the 'ragged Schools' for the children of the poor, became one of the two ministers at Greyfriars in 1836. Typhus raged during his first year, but 'it was not disease or death, it was the starvation, the drunkenness, the rags, the heartless, hopeless miserable condition of the people – the debauched and drunken mothers, the sallow, yellow, emaciated children – their wants, both temporal and spiritual, which one felt themselves unable to relieve – that sometimes overwhelmed me'.

That was the reality on the underside of things. It might induce despair in even the most philanthropic of observers. Dr Bell cried out:

> What can we do? We return day after day, and night after night, to the scenes of misery, disease and death. We listen to the cry of the children, the wail of women, and the deep utterances of men. This awful harmony is in keeping with the picture before us. The pathos of the drama is profound. What can we do? Can we feed the children, comfort the women, and impart hope to the men?

Too often the answer was no.

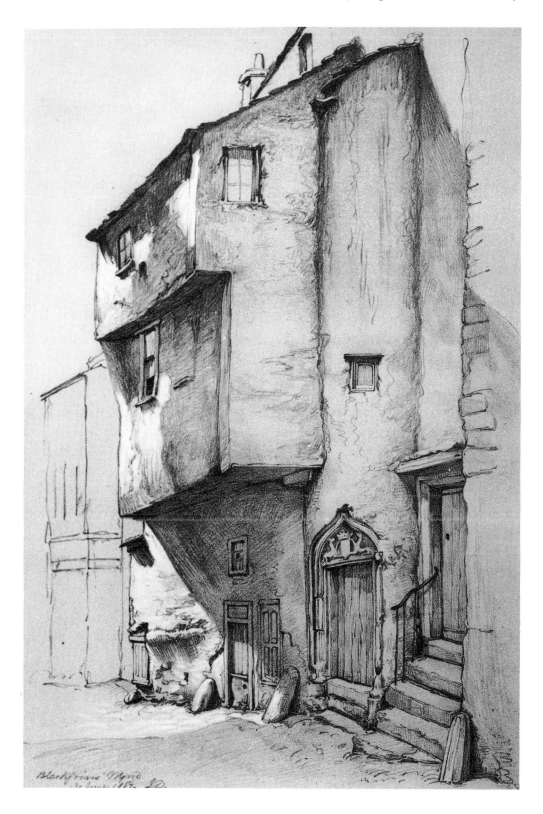

Blackfriars Wynd
16 June 1854. JD.

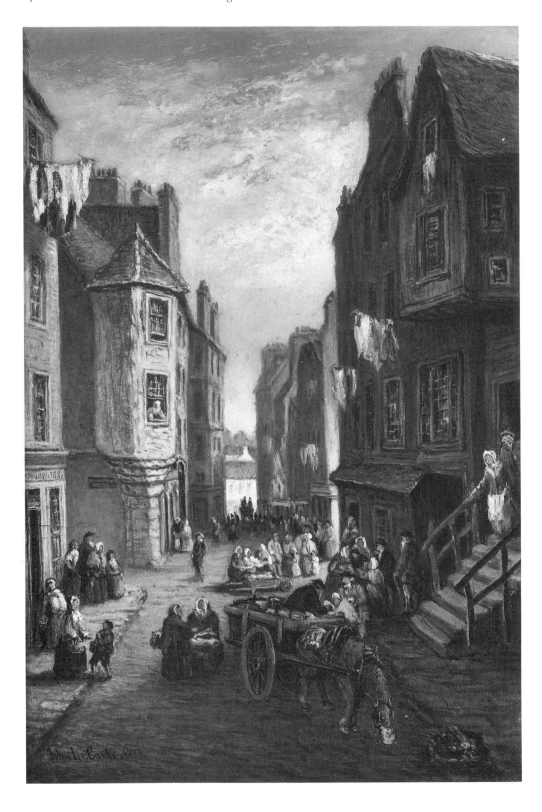

The Cowgate with Cardinal Beaton's House (at the foot of Blackfriars' Wynd) by John le Conte, 1883

Even twenty years later, the magazine *The Builder* decided that every visitor to Edinburgh would carry away two memories: 'a sense of its extraordinary beauty and a horror of its unspeakable filth':

> We devoutly believe that no smell in Europe or Asia – not in Aleppo or Damascus in the present day – can equal in depth and intensity, in concentration and power, the diabolical combination of sulphurated hydrogen we came upon one evening about ten o'clock in a place called Toddick's Wynd.

There was only one way out for most of the unfortunate inhabitants of such places: intoxication leading to oblivion.

'From the toothless infant,' Bell reported, 'to the toothless old man, the population of the wynds drinks whisky. The

'Very fou': engraving by Walter Geikie

drunken drama that is enacted on Saturday night and Sabbath morning beggars description. It is impossible to say how much is expended on the chronic drinking, or everyday consumption, of whisky; and how much on the weekly exacerbation, or grand infernal orgie.'

Nevertheless he tried to do so. In an analysis of Blackfriars Wynd he calculated that if every one of its 1,025 inhabitants drank four gallons of whisky a year (just over a pint a week for each person over the age of fourteen) it would cost the inhabitants of the wynd a sum total of £2,050 a year: but the average lawful income of the wynd was only five pounds a head, or £5,125 in total a year. Of this sum, he calculated that £3,897 would go on food and £650 on rent – to say nothing of charges for fuel and clothing. The books could only be balanced by criminal activity – prostitution and theft: 'If we learnt that they yield £2,000 a year to the wynd, it would in no degree surprise us.'

Prostitution certainly flourished. In 1842 a young doctor, William Tait, published a report in which he calculated that there were at least eight hundred full-time prostitutes in Edinburgh. About a quarter of them lived, as he put it, 'privately', the remainder were to be found in some two hundred brothels, mainly in the Old Town. (Not exclusively so, for the little streets in the New Town also housed brothels, Clyde Street just off St Andrews Square being notorious.) In addition Tait estimated that there were at least 1,200 part-timers whom he called 'sly prostitutes'. Most were very young. Of those treated between 1835 and 1840 for veneral disease at Edinburgh Lock Hospital, 4 per cent were under fifteen, some as young as nine or ten, and 66 per cent were in their late teens.

In 1869 the famous traveller Isabella Bird wrote an account of a return visit to her native city. She visited a brothel and found a room about twelve feet square, divided by rotting partitions, the floor strewn with ashes from the grate, and the only furniture a bed with a straw mattress, a table and a stool:

A girl of about eighteen, very poorly dressed, was sitting on the stool; two others, older and very much undressed, were sitting on the floor, and the three were eating, in the most swinish fashion, out of a large black pot containing fish. I have shared a similar meal in similar primitive fashion in an Indian wigwam in Hudson's Bay Territory, but the women who worshipped the Great Spirit were modest in their dress and manner, and looked *human*, which these 'Christian' young women did not.

An Act of Parliament in 1862 empowered councils to close brothels and drive prostitutes from the streets. It was only partially successful, perhaps because there was no great will among the police to enforce it.

William Logan, author of *The Great Social Evil* (1871), estimated that the number of brothels in Edinburgh had fallen to eighty-five, and considered that the business was conducted 'with less ostentation and attractiveness to the outside world'. It is difficult to know; the brothels may after all have been bigger. Certainly prostitution was bound to flourish as long as poverty drove girls on to the streets and respectable girls were expected to enter marriage as virgins.

Within a few years of Logan's work, the young Robert Louis Stevenson was dallying with the prostitutes who frequented the bars at the top of Leith Walk and in the Old Town. There has been much argument among his biographers as to whether he had a prolonged affair with one, identified as both 'Claire' and 'Kate Drummond'. The balance of probability is in favour of such a relationship. As a recent biographer, Frank McLynn, has written, 'It would fit what we know of RLS's sympathy for the underdog, his quixotry, his toying with "rescue fantasies", his strong feeling for women and the attraction he felt for redemption through suffering.' I find this convincing. Some of his encounters were less happy: one gave him syphilis. He writes of 'the unblushing daughters of Venus' who 'did me a lasting injury'.

10

Victorian Edinburgh

Scott died in 1832, the year of the Reform Act. (Hogg thought the 'Whig ascendancy in the British cabinet' the cause of his death.) Cockburn, as Solicitor-General, and Jeffrey, as Lord Advocate, were responsible for the Scottish version of reform. Cockburn described their intention, in his *Life of Jeffrey*, as that of bringing Scotland 'within the action of the constitution'. Other contingent reforms followed: municipal reform involving the reconstruction of that 'Venetian oligarchy' that had governed Edinburgh. It was all necessary; but Cockburn found, to his regret, that the distinctiveness of Edinburgh was passing away. The Court of Session was reformed, and the Whigs found that Scott had not been so far out; little by little, what made Scotland Scotland was being whittled away. 'Troia fuit,' Scott wrote in his journal as reform loomed.

Carlyle left the city, left Scotland, settled in Chelsea, to become the cynosure of intellectual fashion, but in London, not Edinburgh. There he brooded on the barbarisms of the French Revolution, and on its necessity; on the wickedness of the industrial system, the miseries it caused, the destruction of communities. They were all Scotch themes, but it was the English who responded most to *Past and Present* (1843) in which he developed them, contrasting the state of things today with the records of the medieval monk Jocelin de Brakelond. Spurred by Carlyle, English writers wrote novels about the 'Condition of England', divided as Disraeli said in *Sybil*, into two nations, 'the rich and the poor'. Scotland and Edinburgh had other concerns.

Edinburgh was developing itself as a centre for Romantic

tourism. Curiously this went hand in hand with the continued destruction of the Old Town. The Tolbooth had been removed in 1817 (Scott secured a great iron chest for Abbotsford). The antiquarian Charles Kirkpatrick Sharpe observed 'under the place where the iron box had stood, a number of skeletons of rats, as dry as mummies'. Sharpe protested at a plan to build a new barracks within the castle: 'I have lived,' he wrote, 'to see in the course of 40 years, the Old Town lose much of its primitive features from unavoidable decay, from the rage for *improvement* and the less destructive elements of fire; though I have beheld Salisbury Crags irretrievably injured and Calton Hill utterly destroyed, yet never did I expect to see such a bold attack as this upon the rock of the castle in Edinburgh.'

In this attitude Sharpe showed himself typical of all lovers of the city, for whom every change was for the worse. It would surprise him to know that the destruction of Calton Hill, presumably by the building of the National Monument and that commemorating Nelson, would now be defended as an integral part of the essential Edinburgh skyline, and that any proposal to demolish the castle barracks would be denounced as an act of cultural vandalism.

Cockburn would react with the same contempt and fury to proposals to demolish Trinity Hospital and the Trinity College Kirk to make way for Waverley Station. The suggestion that the

Trinity College Church
by R. Carrick (after W. Leith)

kirk might be rebuilt on Calton Hill did not appease him. The whole thing was 'an outrage by sordid traders, virtually consented to by a tasteless city, and sanctioned by an insensible parliament... These people,' he added, 'would remove Pompeii for a railway and tell us they had applied it to better purpose in Dundee.'

But the railway would be built and Waverley Station would come to be loved, and together they would contribute to the ease

below
Waverley Station from the Scott Monument mid 19th century: photograph by Thomas Begbie

opposite
The Scott Monument: late 19th-century photograph

with which tourists flocked to Edinburgh. Arriving there, they could mount from the depths of the station to Princes Street and admire the extraordinary Gothic memorial which the city had raised to Sir Walter Scott, according to the design of a stonemason named George Meikle Kemp, who drew his inspiration from Melrose Abbey.

But before the railway arrived, another royal tourist had visited the city and expressed her fervent approval. Queen Victoria was only twenty-three when she arrived at Granton Pier in the 'Royal George Yacht'. She found Edinburgh 'quite beautiful, totally unlike anything else I have seen; and what is even more, Albert, who has seen so much, says it is unlike anything *he* ever saw; it is so regular, everything built of massive stone, there is not a brick to be seen anywhere. The *High Street*, which is pretty steep, is very fine. Then the castle, situated on that grand rock in the middle of the town, is most striking. On the other side the *Calton Hill*, with the *National Monument*, a building in the Grecian

Queen Victoria visiting Edinburgh Castle: lithograph after A. Maclure

style; *Nelson's Monument*; *Burns' Monument*; the *Gaol*; the *National School* etc; all magnificent buildings.' So much for Sharpe's criticism.

The queen and her husband then retired to Dalkeith Palace where they were guests of the Duke of Buccleuch (Albert remarking that 'many of the people looked like Germans' – high praise, one assumes). Two days later they were in the city again, travelling past Holyrood ('a royal-looking old place') and up the High Street, 'which is a most extraordinary street from the immense height of the houses, most of them being eleven stories high, and different families living in each storey', and up to the castle where they admired the view, 'like a panorama in extent . . . We saw Heriot's Hospital, a beautiful old building, built, in the time of James, by a jeweller, whom Sir Walter Scott has made famous in his *Fortunes of Nigel*.' They examined the regalia of Scotland and viewed the room in which James VI and I was born – 'such a very, very small room, with an old prayer written on the wall'. Then, somewhat alarmed by the pressure of the crowd, but protected from their enthusiasm by the Royal Company of Archers, they drove out to Dalmeny to lunch with the Earl and Countess of Rosebery. On the way back they admired the view of Edinburgh from the road before Leith – 'quite enchanting; it is, as Albert said, "fairy-like" and what you would only imagine as a thing to dream of, or to see in a picture. Albert said he felt sure the Acropolis could not be finer; and I hear they sometimes call Edinburgh "the modern Athens".'

Victoria's transports were naive, even though Albert concurred in them, but she had a gift for the obvious – 'quite enchanting', 'fairy-like, and what you would only imagine as a thing to dream of, or to see in a picture'. That was how Edinburgh presented itself to the world: the sublime example of the picturesque – the Acropolis could not be finer. Cockburn was wise in reaching for Pompeii as a comparison in his rage; Edinburgh had not been destroyed by lava, and then preserved in it; but what had happened to it came to much the same thing. Even Stevenson, when he came to write about his native city, could not give his essay any title other than 'Picturesque Notes'.

Yet Edinburgh still had its moments of drama, and one such

was enacted in May 1843. It was, indeed, the most important day in nineteenth-century Scottish history, for what happened then was nothing less than the division of the national church. What was at issue was the right of congregations to choose their own minister and reject the laird's assumed right to impose one on them. In 1833 the General Assembly of the Church had passed what was known as the Veto Act, which gave presbyteries the authority to reject an unwelcome minister presented to them by the laird. The Court of Session, however, declared this act to be illegal. The matter went to the House of Lords, which upheld the judgement of the Court, and also permitted a minister rejected by the Presbytery of Auchterarder to sue for damages. Things were thus brought to a head when the General Assembly met in St Andrew's Church (now the Church of St Andrew and St George) in George Street.

Cockburn gave an account of that momentous day in the second volume of his journal:

> Dr Welsh, Professor of Church History in the University of Edinburgh, having been Moderator last year, began the proceeding by preaching a sermon before his Grace the Commissioner in the High Church, in which what was going to happen was announced and defended. The Commissioner then proceeded to St Andrew's Church, where the Assembly was to be held. The streets, especially those near the place of meeting, were filled, not so much with the boys who usually gaze at the annual show, as by grave and well-dressed people of the middle rank. According to custom, Welsh took the chair of the Assembly. Their very first act ought to have been to constitute the Assembly of this year by electing a new Moderator. But before this was done, Welsh rose and announced that he and others who had been returned as members held this not to be a free Assembly – that therefore they declined to acknowledge it as a Court of the Church – that they meant to leave the very place, and, as a consequence of this, to abandon the Establishment. In explanation of the grounds of this step he then read a full and clear protest.
>
> As soon as it was read, Dr Welsh handed the paper to the clerk, quitted the chair, and walked away. Instantly, what appeared to be the whole left side of the house rose to follow. Some applause broke from the

spectators, but it checked itself in a moment. 193 members moved off, of whom about 123 were ministers, and about 70 elders. Among these were many upon whose figures the public eye had long been accustomed to rest in reverence. They all withdrew slowly and regularly amidst perfect silence, till that side of the house was nearly empty.

They were joined outside by a large body of adherents, among whom were about 300 clergymen. As soon as Welsh, who wore his Moderator's dress, appeared on the street, and people saw that principle had really triumphed over interest, he and his followers were received with the loudest acclamations. They walked in procession down Hanover Street to Canonmills, where they had secured an excellent hall, through an unbroken mass of cheering people, and beneath innumerable handkerchiefs waving from the windows. But amidst this exultation there was much sadness and many a tear, many a grave face and fearful thought; for no one could doubt that it was with sore hearts that these ministers left the Church, and no thinking man could look on that unexampled scene, and behold that the temple was rent, without pain and forebodings. No spectacle since the Revolution reminded one so forcibly of the Covenanters.

Altogether 474 ministers out of around 1,200 seceded to form the Free Church. Besides Dr Welsh their leaders included the two most celebrated clergymen of the day, Dr Thomas Chalmers and Dr Thomas Guthrie. In his last sermon in Old St John's Guthrie had stated his position:

> We shall give them their stipends, their manses, their glebes, and their churches. These are theirs, and let them make a kirk or a mill of them. But we cannot give up the crown rights of Christ and we cannot give them up our people's privileges.

It was indeed the old Covenanting language, and when the news of secession was brought to the ageing Lord Jeffrey in his library in Moray Place, he, often so timidly conventional in his judgements, declared, 'I am proud of my country. In not another land in the world would such a thing have been done.'

Yet it was both more and less than it seemed. A little more understanding shown by either the seceders or those who remained loyal to the Established Church, or indeed by the government, could have led to reforms which would have made the Disruption unnecessary. Both parties in the Church had overestimated their support. The Moderates (as the Loyalists were called) had believed that no more than two hundred ministers would secede; Chalmers had been confident that as many as seven hundred – more than half the total number of parish ministers – would follow him. A secession on that scale would have made compromise and reconciliation imperative.

In one sense the demands of the seceding Evangelicals were the natural corollary of the parliamentary and municipal reforms already achieved (which perhaps accounts for the enthusiasm shown by Cockburn and Jeffrey), but they were also in the essentially conservative tradition of Scottish Presbyterianism. The Evangelicals looked back to the Covenanting myth and sighed for the lost purity of the religion of the seventeenth-century theocracy, when Scotland was like Israel, a nation obedient to the will of the Almighty. Yet in reality the secession itself diluted that tradition, even though the willingness to sacrifice interest and material well-being to principle seemed at first to fortify it. At a time when the ever-growing urban working class was being lost to organised religion (something of which both Chalmers and Guthrie were keenly aware), the Disruption not only weakened the Established Church of Scotland, which had set out to be, whatever its deficiencies, the Church of the whole nation, but diverted the energies of many Evangelicals to the financing, building and organisation of their own Free Churches in parishes throughout the land. Soon, according to Michael Lynch in his *History of Scotland*, 'its working-class members grew tired of its incessant demand for contributions, however small. The sneer of the Established Church – ''Money! money! money! with the Free Church is everything'' – had some substance to it.'

Yet, in the early days at least, the Free Kirk's missionary zeal was impressive. Guthrie exemplified it. In 1847 he published *A Plea for Ragged Schools* after meeting some poor boys by St Anthony's Well in Holyrood Park; they told him they had never been to school, and he asked them if they would attend one

which also promised them a square meal. He got support from the journalist Hugh Miller, editor of the Free Kirk newspaper *Witness*, and from the Lord Provost of Edinburgh, Adam Black, the publisher of the *Encyclopaedia Britannica* and later (1856–65) Liberal MP for the city. By the end of that year (1847) three charity schools had been established; they were attended by more than 250 children. The Governor of Edinburgh Prison added his support when he realised that the number of children consigned to his charge had dropped considerably. Even so, such schools could only serve a tiny minority of those who needed them. Guthrie, himself strongly in favour of compulsory education, had raised £116,000 in eleven months (1845–6) for the provision of Free Church manses; that was far more than he could persuade the public to subscribe for his Ragged Schools.

Guthrie was also active in the temperance movement, seeing the easy availability of alcohol as a cause of poverty and crime. He became a total abstainer himself – ten years after its foundation about a hundred Free Kirk ministers had taken the pledge of abstinence. (There were only about twenty abstaining ministers in the Established Church, and the leader of the Scottish Temperance League complained that the chief business of its General Assembly 'seems to be the deposition of her ministers for the sin of drunkenness'.) The reformers had some success. The Forbes-Mackenzie Act of 1853 shut the pubs on Sundays (though *bona fide* travellers could still get a drink at hotels with a seven-day licence) and imposed a closing time of 11 p.m. The Police Superintendent of Leith, which as a port was famous for drunkenness, thought that 'the Act has done good – and created evil – while it has diminished drunkenness and tended to the better observance of the Sabbath, it has brought into existence and fostered illicit trafficking in spirits.' But the better observance of the Sabbath was much approved by the Free Kirk, in Edinburgh as elsewhere. Duncan McLaren, Black's successor as Lord Provost and Liberal MP, and a member of an earlier secessionist church, the United Presbyterians, was an abstainer himself, but as Lord Provost did not feel able to ban liquor from his table – a decent, very Edinburgh compromise.

McLaren was the dominant figure in Edinburgh, indeed

Temperance Hotel in the High Street
in the house which once belonged to Allan Ramsay

Scottish, politics in the mid-century. Born in Dumbartonshire in 1800, he set up as a draper in Edinburgh, and entered municipal politics. As treasurer in the 1830s he took measures which saved the city from the threat of bankruptcy. Married to a sister of the English radical John Bright, he was the incarnation of the Victorian principles of self-help, thrift and self-sufficiency. He joined his brother-in-law in opposing the Corn Laws. He organised a convention of dissenting ministers which declared the laws 'alike opposed to the principles of religion and the precepts of morality'. (By keeping the price of bread artificially high, the Corn Laws also kept wages above the level which employers considered economically necessary, or indeed just.) McLaren himself denounced the historian Lord Macaulay, who was then MP for Edinburgh but who hesitated to advocate reform, for being 'against the enlightened opinion of the middle class', which McLaren, fairly enough, took himself to represent. Twenty years later he was in the vanguard of the movement for the Second Reform Bill, seeking a six-pound franchise to extend the vote to industrious artisans, who could be relied on to vote Liberal. He was opposed to most corporate activity, and to the domination of Scottish politics by the legal establishment. Urging Gladstone in 1869 to appoint an Under-Secretary of State at the Home Office with responsibility for Scottish affairs, he argued that 'there is a feeling among many who have no connection with Edinburgh, that Edinburgh and its lawyers rule everything, and there is a strong feeling of jealousy on the part of many. At present no man, let his talents be what they may, can ever be Minister for Scotland, unless he becomes not merely a lawyer, but a successful lawyer, and gets to the head of his profession. Then he may retain office for a long term of years, thus stopping all promotion.' No doubt the fact that he was not himself a lawyer, and thus ineligible for the position of Lord Advocate, through whom all Scottish government business was channelled, fuelled his indignation.

But if McLaren was opposed to the privileged position of the legal establishment, he was equally hostile to the pretensions of organised labour: 'He detested the idea that workers might be given statutory privilege in pursuing their disputes, just as he

Duncan McLaren
by Edward John Gregory

had always detested statutory privileges for the Kirk and the landlords.'* As a result of his promotion in 1873 of the Criminal Law Amendment Act, which made picketing illegal, McLaren was denounced as 'a traitor to the working-class interest', at a demonstration in the Queen's Park. The accusation was unjust; he had never been devoted to that cause. He was the Victorian middle class personified.

All the political struggles in mid-nineteenth century Edinburgh took place within the Whig-Liberal-Radical coalition; the Tories were irrelevant, till the end of the century, when the Liberal Party split over Gladstone's proposals to grant Home Rule to Ireland. McLaren himself, in the last year of his life, broke with his party on this issue, coming out in favour of Unionism. It was a moment of symbolic importance. The philosophy which he had incarnated was moribund. The cause of individualism – the conviction that there was no need of intermediary between a man and his Maker – was being swamped by new calls, for social action from both right and left. Even Free Trade would soon be no longer a sacrosanct doctrine; within twenty years of McLaren's death, the former radical leader Joseph Chamberlain would be advocating Protection. The Liberal world of McLaren and Gladstone, so agreeable to middle-class Edinburgh, so much the political equivalent of the Free Kirk, was passing away.

If McLaren had been its essentially representative figure in Edinburgh and Scotland, Gladstone, though far too complicated a man to be catalogued so neatly, had been its inspiration, and in the two Midlothian campaigns of 1880–81 gave Edinburgh its greatest political excitement since the Reform Bill. It was characteristic of Edinburgh and Victorian Scotland that the occasion of these outbursts of extraordinary excitement and enthusiasm should have been a moral issue – the behaviour of Turkish troops in Bulgaria and the refusal of Disraeli's Tory government to condemn the atrocities.

The Midlothian constituency for which Gladstone was standing did not, of course, include the city, and meetings were held throughout it, as well as in the Border towns which he

* Fry, *Patronage and Privilege*.

Dinner at Haddo House by A. E. Emslie, 1884. Gladstone is shown in profile to the right of centre; Lord Rosebery is on the far left

passed through on his journey north by way of the Midland railway, but the highest peaks of excitement were reached in the great public meetings held in Edinburgh and organised by the Earl of Rosebery from his home at Dalmeny a few miles out of the city.

Gladstone arrived in Edinburgh for the first campaign on 24 November 1880. A huge crowd greeted him at Waverley, where Rosebery met him, and then a procession of carriages, with uniformed outriders, made its way through packed streets out of the city to Dalmeny. 'The noise,' Mrs Gladstone wrote, was 'more than deafening, hundreds flying along by the side of the carriage, and the whole way to Dalmeny more or less lined with people and torches and fireworks and bonfires.' Crowds of Liberals roamed the streets all evening looking for an enemy to engage, but the Tories had vanished. 'I have never,' Gladstone said, 'gone through a more extraordinary day.'

That was only the beginning. The next day he addressed a
packed meeting in the Music Hall in George Street before
travelling out to Dalkeith, in the heart of the constituency.
'Several times,' Mrs Gladstone said, 'we went through horrors
from the reckless crowding of the people, pressing on the
carriage, hanging on to the wheels, such pinched eager faces.'
Edinburgh, Midlothian, Scotland indeed had never experienced
such political enthusiasm, at least since the seventeenth century.
On the 29th Gladstone was back in the capital, speaking to a
crowd of more than twenty thousand in the Waverley Market.
Rosebery found it 'a strange sight. Gladstone calmly perorating
about Bulgaria while the fainting people were lifted over pale and
motionless into the reporters' enclosure. He felt it though he did
not show it and spoke for barely twenty minutes. A frightful
business getting back to the carriage through the mob.'

The second campaign in the spring saw similar scenes of
enthusiasm.

Edinburgh did not become an industrial city like Glasgow or
Dundee. It continued to be dominated by the professions, the law
especially, and the University. The decay of the Old Town
continued despite attempts by William Chambers, Lord Provost
from 1865 to 1869, to revive it. He restored St Giles Cathedral at
his own expense, and was responsible for the construction of
George IV Bridge and the street named after him, which together
did something to open the upper portion of the Old Town and so
render it more agreeable. (The Architectural Institute of Scotland
actually recommended that the whole of the Old Town should be
demolished and rebuilt.)

The renovations stimulated by Chambers, along with the
building of the Royal Infirmary and the Royal Scottish Museum,
the Dental Hospital and the James Watt Institute, meant that the
upper portion of the Old Town lying between the High Street and
George Square, and bounded to the east by the line of the
bridges, became a sort of educational quarter with fine public
buildings. But the decay of the Canongate and the Cowgate and
Grassmarket continued, as they sank into ever deeper squalor and
disrepair. Quite early in Victoria's reign Cockburn had lamented

Interior of Parliament House,
1851

the dereliction of St Cecilia's Hall in the Cowgate. It had been:

> . . . the best and most beautiful concert room I have ever
> yet seen. And there have I myself seen most of our
> literary and fashionable gentlemen, predominating with
> their side curls, and frills and ruffles, and silver buckles;
> and our stately matrons stiffened in hoops, and gorgeous
> satin; and our beauties with high-heeled shoes, powdered
> and pomatomed hair, and lofty and composite head
> dresses. All this was in the Cowgate! the last retreat
> nowadays of destitution and disease. The building still
> stands, though raised and changed, and is looked down
> upon from South Bridge, over the eastern side of the
> Cowgate Arch. When I last saw it, it seemed to be partly
> an old-clothesman's shop, and partly a brazier's. The
> abolition of this Cecilian temple, and the necessity of
> finding accommodation where they could, and of
> depending for patronage on the common boisterous
> public, of course extinguished the delicacies of the old
> artificial parterre.

It might have cheered him to know that more than a century later
the hall would be restored by the University and be in regular use
for concerts during the Festival.

Of course there was some industry in Edinburgh. It was a
centre of brewing and printing, and remained the second most
important publishing centre in Britain. The railway had come in
1842, and almost the only major Edinburgh industrialist and
entrepreneur, Sir James Gowans, started his working life as a
railway engineer, eventually in 1886 being responsible for
Edinburgh's only attempt at an International Exhibition of
Industry, Science and Art, in a temporary hall set up in the
Meadows. It was perhaps appropriate, however, that the hall's
designer came from Glasgow. For the most part, industrial
Edinburgh was a city of artisan workshops rather than factories.
It already showed a preference for engaging in white-collar
business like banks and life assurance companies; Edinburgh
may even lay claim to having invented modern banking and
modern life insurance.

Labourers and artisans might be accommodated in the drab
tenements that spread up the Dalry and Gorgie Roads from
Haymarket Station or in Easter Road running parallel to Leith

*Chambers Street, South Bridge
and George IV Bridge*

Walk from the north-east end of the Calton Hill, but though these might quickly degenerate into slums, they could not be compared to the awfulness of contemporary Glasgow or Dundee. The most conspicuous feature of Edinburgh's development in the Victorian Age was its spread to the south and west: huge tenement blocks for the middle and lower middle classes in Marchmont, Bruntsfield, dignified terraces extending west of Charlotte Square and across the Dean Bridge, handsome villas in gardens with laburnum and lilac in Grange, Morningside and Colinton. These might be deplored by traditionalists – Robert Louis Stevenson among them – and certainly they represented a retreat from the old ways of communal living. There was even something English about them – a criticism that would be advanced still more forcibly in the twentieth century when the bungalow became the characteristic form of detached or semi-detached house. But the criticism was excessive. The great men of the Enlightenment – or at least of its later phase – like Jeffrey and Cockburn had delighted in their rural retreats on the fringes of the city. Jeffrey had his little estate, his Horatian villa, on Corstorphine Hill, Cockburn his Bonaly Tower in the foothills of the Pentlands. What was now being built for the well-to-do of Edinburgh was intended to offer them the same delight of *rus in urbe*. The richer among them, in the years before the First World War tore things apart, enjoyed something of that 'sweetness of life' which Talleyrand had ascribed to the time before the revolution in France. Lord Boothby, the Unionist MP for East Aberdeenshire for thirty-four years, born in 1900 and brought up in a villa called Beechwood on Corstorphine Hill, recalled that 'Edinburgh was surrounded by ducal palaces and large mansions designed and adorned by the Adam brothers, inhabited for the most part by baronets. My parents were far from affluent; but I remember no period before the second world war when we had less than six indoor servants, two gardeners and a chauffeur.' Affluence is, of course, comparative; his father, Sir Tom Boothby, was General Manager of the Scottish Provident Insurance Company.

Yet as with all proud nineteenth-century cities, Edinburgh's finest buildings of this period were public institutions of one kind or another. This is something we have lost: that civic zeal that

opposite
International Exhibition, 1886. 'Old Edinburgh' exhibit – reconstruction of the Mercat Cross and Old Assembly Rooms

overleaf
Bruntsfield Place: Victorian tenements

The National Gallery of Scotland and the Royal Scottish Academy from the Scott Monument: photograph by George Washington Wilson, c. 1870

Bank of Scotland, the Mound perspective by David Bryce of his proposed building

Fettes College
by David Bryce

expresses itself in grandeur and beauty, created in the desire to do good and leave often a record of the founder's magnanimity. It was a time of great architects, too. Playfair, London-born and a pupil of Wyatt, the Prince Regent's favourite architect, was a master of many styles: classical (the Royal Scottish Academy, the National Gallery and Surgeon's Hall), Jacobean (Donaldson's Hospital), sixteenth-century Gothic (the Free Church College). Thomas Hamilton was a master of the Greek style, modelling his Royal High School on the Temple of Theseus in Athens, though he never visited Greece himself. David Bryce, the pre-eminent favourite of the Scottish banks in the mid-century, evolved the Scottish baronial style, which owed much to memories of the *châteaux* of the Loire Valley. His headquarters of the Bank of Scotland on the Mound perfectly expresses the confidence of the banking establishment. Bryce's most extraordinary, fanciful and yet successful building is Fettes College, derided by many who in time came to admire it keenly. Comparable to Fettes was the Renaissance extravagance of Daniel Stewart's College, built some fifteen years earlier, which also contrives to recall the Pavilion at Brighton.

11

Stevenson and Edinburgh

No one gives the flavour of Victorian Edinburgh, catches its very smell, sound and moral atmosphere, better than Stevenson. Little of his fiction is set in the city of his birth, or at least not ostensibly so; yet Stevenson is the essential Edinburgh writer, far more so than Scott, whose heart was in the Borders. Stevenson is

Heriot Row

both charming and stern, like Edinburgh itself. He is Calvinist and Romantic, a rebel against convention and Presbyterian morality, and yet at the same time imbued with it. The man who wrote 'There are no rights and plenty duties' spoke the language of Chalmers and Guthrie.

He was born in Howard Place, in Inverleith, across the road from the Botanic Gardens. He was the son of a family of engineers who had built most of the lighthouses around the coasts of Scotland, and all his life had a sense of inferiority and guilt because he had taken a different route. The house in Howard Place was small and damp, too near the Water of Leith, polluted by the effluent from a nearby tannery, for a delicate child, and in 1857 the Stevensons removed to the grander address of Heriot Row. It was there that Louis grew up, struggling against the chronic ill-health which cut short his schooling at the Edinburgh Academy down the hill – to his satisfaction. It was from memories of Heriot Row and holidays at the manse of Colinton, where his

Colinton Manse

maternal grandfather was minister, that he later made *The Child's Garden of Verses* with its evocation of winter afternoons when the lamplighter lit the gas-lamps in the street, while the small boy looked out of the window and waited for his tea. 'The delicate die early,' was his memory of Edinburgh winters, 'and I, as a survivor among bleak winds and plumping rain, have been sometimes tempted to envy them their fate.' Yet he survived, just as he survived the Scottish Sabbath when 'prayers came at the same hour, the Sabbath literature was unimpeachably selected . . . and over which there reigned all week, and grew denser on Sundays, a silence . . . and a gloom'.

In 1867 he began to attend the University. He did so only fitfully, for he had no desire to become an engineer (his first course of study) or a lawyer (his second). Nevertheless the University left a profound impression on him.

> The English lad goes to Oxford or Cambridge; then, in an ideal world of gardens, to live in a semi-scenic life, costumed, disciplined, and drilled by proctors . . . At an earlier age the Scottish lad begins his greatly different experience, of crowded class-rooms, of a gaunt quadrangle, of a bell hourly booming over the traffic of the city to recall him from the public-house where he has been lunching or the streets where he has been wandering fancy-free. His college life has little of restraint, and nothing of necessary gentility . . . All classes rub shoulders on the greasy benches. The raffish young gentleman in gloves must measure his scholarship with the plain, clownish laddie from the parish school. They separate at the session's end, one to smoke cigars about a watering-place, the other to resume the labours of the field beside his peasant family.

The young Stevenson spent more time, however, in the streets and public houses than in the lecture room. Because his family kept him short of money, he frequented the cheapest and most disreputable taverns in Leith Street, the Cowgate and the Canongate. 'I was the companion,' he said, 'of seamen, chimney-sweeps and thieves; my circle was being continually changed by the action of the police magistrate.' He enjoyed the company of prostitutes, off-duty at least. In an unpublished paper, he

The Horsefair in the Grass Market
by James Howe

Warriston's Close by Henry Duguid.
The contrast between the Old and New Towns
is exemplified by the sight of the gleaming
monument to Lord Melville (erected 1821)
in St Andrew Square beyond the crumbling
houses off the High Street

William Burke
('The Murderer')
and *William Hare*
('King's Evidence'):
contemporary
prints from
Wretch's Illustrations

The Port of Leith with a distant view of Edinburgh by Paul Jean Clays

The Revd Thomas Guthrie on a Mission of Mercy by James Edgar

Robert Louis Stevenson
by Count Girolamo Nerli

Edinburgh Old and New by David Octavius Hill

View of the Lawnmarket by W. G. Herdman

Tea Room
by Stanley Cursiter,
1913

North Bridge and Salisbury Crags from the Northwest by Adam Bruce Thomson

Edinburgh (from Salisbury Crags) by William Crozier, 1927

described one as 'a robust, great-haunched, blue-eyed young woman, of admirable temper, and, if you will let me say so of a prostitute, extraordinary modesty.' In periods of respectability she would work in a factory or shop, and then she would refuse to acknowledge him if they encountered each other on Leith Walk.

R. L. Stevenson in Barrister's Robes

Wandering about the slum quarters of the city excited his imagination:

One night I went along the Cowgate after everyone was a-bed but the policeman, and stopped by hazard before a

The Canongate with Jenny Ha's
Changehouse (a tavern):
photograph by Thomas
Begbie, c. 1850

tall land. The moon touched upon its chimneys and shone blankly on the upper windows. There was no light anywhere in the great bulk of the building; but as I stood there, it seemed to me that I could hear quite a body of quiet sounds from the interior; doubtless there were many clocks ticking; and people snoring on their backs. And, thus, as I fancied, the dense life within made itself faintly audible in my ears, family after family contributing its quota to the general hum, and the whole pile beating in tune to its time-pieces, like a great disordered heart. Perhaps it was little more than a fancy altogether, but it was strangely impressive at the time, and gave me an imaginative measure of the disproportion between the quantity of living flesh and the trifling walls that separated and contained it.

No doubt such a passage could have been written about any city, yet the picture of the young Stevenson, shivering in his velvet coat, as he stood by that tenement, which had once perhaps been the home of some noble family in the Cowgate, and breathing in the sense of an abundance of sleeping life, as the moon stood over Arthur's Seat, is not only incomparably vivid, but somehow belongs very completely to his particular Edinburgh, and the vision he had of it. For Stevenson, as for Hogg, Edinburgh was a city held in the grip of a dual identity: respectable and God-fearing on the one hand, rebellious and scornful in its debauchery on the other. It was not just that the city was physically clearly divided between its two antipathetic quarters. The duality was more subtle than that; it was contained within the breast of every individual. This was why Stevenson was so drawn to the story of Deacon Brodie. It was because of this sensation that he came to write that masterpiece of dual personality, *The Strange Case of Dr Jekyll and Mr Hyde*, the strangest feature of which is that it is ostensibly set in London, not Edinburgh. Yet no one who knows Edinburgh has ever doubted that it is an essentially Edinburgh story.

It was by this time about nine in the morning, and the first fog of the season. A great chocolate-coloured pall lowered over heaven but the wind was continually charging and routing these embattled vapours [that is Edinburgh surely] so that as the cab crawled from street to street, Mr Utterson beheld a marvellous number of degrees and hues of twilight; for here it would be dark like the back-end of evening; and light of some strange conflagration; and here, for a moment, the fog would be broken up, and a haggard shaft of daylight would glance in between the swirling wreaths.

So exactly is Edinburgh evoked that it still comes as a shock to find that the next sentence brings us to 'the dismal quarter of Soho'.

When, in his will, Dr Jekyll refers to his evil double Hyde as 'my friend and benefactor', and yet at the end writes, 'Half an hour from now, when I shall again and forever reindue that hated personality, I know how I shall sit weeping and shuddering in my chair', can anyone knowing the stories of Edinburgh read this, and not be reminded of Major Weir – Angelical Thomas – and his cry, 'I have lived like a beast, let me die like a beast'?

Stevenson had a clear view of the social divisions in the city. In *Edinburgh: Picturesque Notes*, published in 1878 when he was not yet thirty, he wrote, in a manner that recalls Cockburn's nostalgia for 'the last purely Scotch age' and then takes a sorrowful look at his own:

It is true that over-population was at least as dense in the epoch of lords and ladies, and that nowadays some customs which made Edinburgh notorious of yore have been fortunately praetermitted. [He refers to the habit of hurling excrement and all sort of garbage into the street below with the cry 'Gardyloo'.] But an aggregation of comfort is not distasteful like an aggregation of the reverse. Nobody cares how many lords and ladies, and divines and lawyers, may have been crowded into these houses in the past – perhaps the more the merrier. The glasses clink round the punch-bowl, some one touches the virginals, there are peacocks' feathers on the chimney, and the tapers burn clear and pale in the red firelight. That is not an ugly picture in itself, nor will it become ugly on repetition. All the better if the like were going on in every second room; the land would only look the more inviting. Times are changed. In one house, perhaps two-score families herd together; and perhaps, not one of them is wholly out of reach of want. The great hotel is given over to discomfort from the foundations to the chimney-tops; everywhere a pinching, narrow habit,

Advocates Close:
etching by Fitton Hedley

scant meals and an air of sluttishness and dirt. In the first
room there is a birth, in another a death, in a third a sordid
drinking bout, and the detective and the Bible-reader cross
upon the stairs. High words are audible from dwelling to
dwelling, and children have a strange experience from the
first; only a robust soul, you would think, could grow up in
such conditions without hurt. And even if God tempers his
dispensations to the young, and all the ill does not arise in
the way that our apprehensions may forecast, the sight of
such a way of living is disquieting to people who are more
happily circumstanced. Social inequality is nowhere more
ostentatious than at Edinburgh. I have mentioned already
how, to the stroller along Princes Street, the High Street
callously exhibits its back garrets. It is true, there is a garden
in between. And although nothing could be more glaring by
way of contrast, sometimes the opposition is more
immediate; sometimes the thing lies in a nutshell, and there
is not so much as a blade of grass between the rich and the
poor. To look over the South Bridge and see the Cowgate
below full of crying hawkers, is to view one rank of society
from another in the twinkling of an eye.

The contrast depressed him. The rectitude of the 'unco guid',
among whom at times he was compelled to number his otherwise
much-loved father, exasperated him. There were occasions when
he could hardly wait to get away from the place, and thought that
the passengers on a south-bound train from Waverley were the
most fortunate of beings: 'Happy the passengers who shake off
the dust of Edinburgh and have heard for the last time the cry of
the east wind among her chimney-tops.' Even then, however, he
paused, for 'the place establishes an interest in people's hearts;
go where they will, they take a pride in their city'.

In that mood of pride he could extol it as fervently as any of
its uncritical lovers:

It is as much a matter of course to decry the New Town as
to exalt the Old; and the most celebrated authorities [he
was probably thinking of Ruskin first of all, who had
complained of the 678 identical windows of Queen Street
'altogether void of any relief by decoration'] have picked
out this quarter as the very emblem of what is
condemnable in architecture. [How fashions change!]
Much may be said, much indeed has been said, upon the
text; but to the unsophisticated, who call anything

pleasing if only it pleases them, the New Town of
Edinburgh seems, in itself, not only gay and airy, but highly
picturesque . . . There are bright and temperate days –
with soft air coming from the inland hills, military music
sounding bravely from the hollow of the gardens, the flags
all waving on the palaces of Princes Street – when I have
seen the town through a sort of glory . . . On such a day, the
valley wears a surprising air of festival. It seems . . . as if it
were a trifle too good to be true. It is what Paris ought to be.
It has the scenic quality that would best set off a life of
unthinking open-air diversion. It was meant by nature for
the realization of the society of comic operas. And you can
imagine, if the climate were but towardly, how all the world
and his wife would flock into these gardens in the cool of the
evening, to hear cheerful music, to sip pleasant drinks, to
see the moon rise behind Arthur's Seat, and shine upon the
spires and monuments and the green tree-tops in the valley.

This is the Edinburgh that many today have known during its
Festival, and it seems almost as if Stevenson had miraculously
anticipated it.

'Alas!' he continues, 'and the next morning the rain is
splashing on the window, and the passengers flee along Princes
Street before the galloping squalls' – a sentence that captures the
emptiness many citizens feel when the Festival packs its tents
and is over for another year, leaving Edinburgh to the swiftly
advancing gales of autumn and the chill of its northern winter.

Stevenson picks out another reason for Edinburgh's scenic
magnificence and its ability continually to surprise even those
who know the city well. Nowhere else, he says, in no other city
'does the sight of the country enter so far . . . The place if full of
theatre tricks in the way of scenery. You peep under an arch, you
descend stairs that look as if they would land you in a cellar, you
turn to the back window of a grimy tenement in a lane: – and
behold! you are face to face with distant and bright prospects.
You turn a corner, and there is the sun going down into the
Highland hills. You look down an alley and see ships tacking for
the Baltic.'

The ships today are more likely to be oil tankers on their way
to or from Grangemouth where they discharge their cargo, but
the surprise and delight remain. To front George Street on a clear

bright morning and see the Firth of Forth beyond you and the hills of Fife on the further bank is to share Stevenson's relish in his city. He never lost that feeling. Exile indeed sharpened it.

In the manuscript of *Weir of Hermiston*, the novel on which he was working when he died, his widow Fanny found some verses addressed to her; the opening lines testify to the pains of exile. Their nostalgia touches anyone who has loved Edinburgh:

> I saw rain falling and the rainbow drawn
> On Lammermuir. Hearkening I heard again
> In my precipitous city beaten bells
> Winnow the keen sea wind. And here afar
> From my own race and place I wrote . . .

12

The Years to 1914

In the last decades of the nineteenth century Edinburgh yielded pride of place to Glasgow; two great International Exhibitions held in Kelvingrove Park in 1888 and 1901 far surpassed the one Sir James Gowans had organised in Edinburgh in 1886, and confirmed Glasgow's claim to be 'the Second City of the Empire'. In comparison with the zest and vitality of Glasgow, Edinburgh seemed to sleep. Its citizens responded by dismissing Glasgow as 'vulgar'; 'typical Edinburgh way of doing business' was the

Edinburgh in 1886: engraving after H. W. Brewer & T. Griffiths

response of a Glasgow lawyer in Buchan's *Huntingtower*, when an Edinburgh colleague was unable to give a straight and immediate answer to a question. Moreover, in Charles Rennie Mackintosh Glasgow had an architect who was recognised in Europe at least as a master of the New Art which the Viennese called *Jugendstil*. Edinburgh, in contrast, seemed content to live on the memory of its glorious past.

Cable Tram at Church Hill

It lived, at least as far as the middle classes were concerned, in great comfort. An excellent tramcar system carried them from Morningside or Colinton, Murrayfield or Grange, clanking down Lothian Road or across the bridges, to shops and offices, to Princes Street with its fine department stores and innumerable tea-rooms, and back in the evening to substantial high teas or, for the professional classes, dinners. Their world was solid, in-curious, permanent. They took their holidays in the Highlands or on the coasts of the Moray Firth, Fife or East Lothian. The gentlemen played golf, and the ladies . . . well, it was sometimes hard to know how the ladies filled their days, but there was no doubt they did so pleasantly. The family attended the Kirk on the Sabbath, but were for the most part careful not to allow the more difficult demands of the Christian religion to disturb the even tenor of existence.

The mood of Edinburgh and of much of Scotland was nostalgic. Small town and village Scotland were celebrated in the writings of the Kailyard novelists – J. M. Barrie, S. R. Crockett, and John Watson (who wrote as Ian McLaren), all graduates of Edinburgh University. Even more popular was Annie S. Swan (1859–1943), author of countless light romantic novels, educated at the Queen Street Ladies' College (subsequently Mary Erskine's School for Girls); she wrote her first novels living in a flat in Morningside while her husband was a medical student. It was appropriate; Edinburgh was in some respects at least merely the largest small town in Scotland.

Of course it was not quite so simple. The comfortable middle class might live in happy oblivion of the darker and harsher aspects of the city with which – to be fair to them – they scarcely came in contact, for the poor rarely ventured into the New Town, and the well-to-do had no cause to penetrate the Cowgate.

Occasionally, however, they might be forced to take some cognisance of the way the poor lived. There was one such occasion in the winter of 1888–9. It concerned a wretched woman, Jessie King, who was accused of the murder of three infant children. There was little doubt that she was guilty (though perhaps of culpable homicide, it might now be decided, rather than murder); there was little doubt either that her companion, a hefty brute called Pearson (sometimes Macpherson) was equally guilty; but to secure a conviction against the woman he was permitted to turn Queen's Evidence. The three murdered chil-dren were all the offspring of unmarried servant girls, who, to keep their situations, were compelled to farm out their babies, or pay someone to take them on. That was Jessie King's role, and

The Life History of a Slum Child.

"This is "a nameless lassie"
nursed by her unhappy mother's
unhappier mother in a
room which was not untypical
& which contained.

A chair-bed with old coats for covering.

A chair.

A box for a second seat.

A table.

A lamp.

A pot & kettle.

A strip of old worn-out carpet.

A few dishes & odd (indeed odd!)
    ornaments (sic).

And literally Nothing else.

This was the <u>HOME</u> of the father (who
was in prison when the child was born)
& the Mother who was just <u>16</u> years of age.

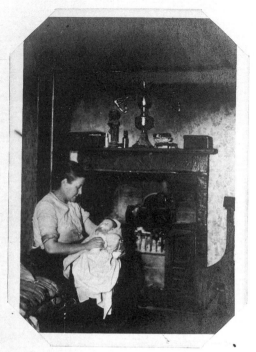

Those are, not the
actual parents of this
child, but others of the
same class & age –
irresponsible, self-indulgent
-bold - to whom alas
too often, Love . . . .
is the lamp of the
tomb."

'The Life History of a Slum Child':
photographs and text by the founders of St Saviour's Child Garden, Chessel Court, c. 1900

she then killed them either through incompetence, or to save the money she had been paid. It was a mean and sordid little story, but it said something about morality, for the servant girls were all in positions in respectable households, and it was indeed the respectability which made it impossible for them to keep their babies.

Of course, there were only three in the case, and domestic servants abounded – the census of 1881 revealed that 20 per cent of the population of Edinburgh was employed in domestic services. Even so, this revelation of a callous trade in unwanted infants was disquieting. *The Scotsman* pondered the matter. 'In Foreign countries,' the leader writer opined, ' – in Naples for instance, there are Foundling Institutions where deserted children, the offspring in most cases of guilty passions are cared for and brought up.' Yet, he considered, this was hardly a satisfactory answer. Might not the existence of such institutions serve as a support of vice? Even as an encouragement? For who would feel the need of continence and chastity if they knew that there was a Foundling Hospital ready to receive and rear the fruits of sin? So there was perhaps nothing to be done except preach morality.

There were still, however, a few who saw it as their mission to disturb the complacency even of Edinburgh. One such was Patrick Geddes (1854–1932), frequently described as a polymath. In fact he was trained as a biologist, made himself a sociologist, and can fairly be called the father of town planning, at least in Scotland. He believed that the lessons derived from the study of animal biology could usefully be applied to human society (a proposition of doubtful value) and he was indignantly eager to stimulate a revival of Scottish culture, an ambition not divorced from his biological-sociological concerns. He called for a Scottish renascence, and was not loth to claim that he was leading it. He was indeed a remarkable man, and one who had considerable influence; he might have had more if he had written better, but though he is capable of the occasional pungent phrase, much of his writing is vapid and pretentious.

He deplored the way in which Scotland (and with it Edinburgh) were losing what had been distinctive. He wrote to a friend in 1910:

Of this process there is a great instance just now, a loss of the first magnitude. But this, it is some compensation to read, may wake up the community as nothing has ever done before, – the University, City Fathers and all – masters and workmen too, as they grasp its present meaning, and still more its significance for the future. Even West End lawyers will understand it!

What can this be which can rouse our sleeping city, you will ask? Get from your bookseller the prospectus of the *Encyclopaedia Britannica*, now advertised as acquired by the Cambridge University Press, and to be re-edited there in a new [11th] edition.

Now so strangely and fixedly asleep are my fellow-citizens that no one whom I have met since this announcement appeared in the 'Scotsman' lately, has noticed anything more in this than in any other ordinary business transfer; no more indeed than did that great newspaper itself – (all the more evidently our appropriate organ, you will say!) Yet as you know, my acquaintance is not among those whom you would consider the most comatose, but quite otherwise; in fact among the positively or relatively awake and open-minded! And as so far consolatory evidence of this, they have seen as I pointed it out (and so would you have come to see without me,) – what a loss this means a) for the printing trade of Edinburgh in future years, as compared with past ones; also b) for the authority of Edinburgh science, medicine, and other faculties. When we edited or wrote in it from Edinburgh, Cambridge was not left out – witness Ward's great article on Psychology for instance – but who in Cambridge will come to Edinburgh.

Geddes here struck a note which would be sounded repeatedly throughout the twentieth century; and yet the letter offers hints also, why for all his gifts, he achieved so much less than he hoped for. His contempt for others was too clear and too pervasive. However, by the time he wrote this letter, he had some reason for feeling disappointed and undervalued.

Early on he had seized on Stevenson's *Picturesque Notes* and echoed them:

The upper and middle classes have been wont to traverse old Edinburgh by viaducts high above the festering squalor below, and to live and die in practical indifference

Sir Patrick Geddes
by Desmond Chute, 1930

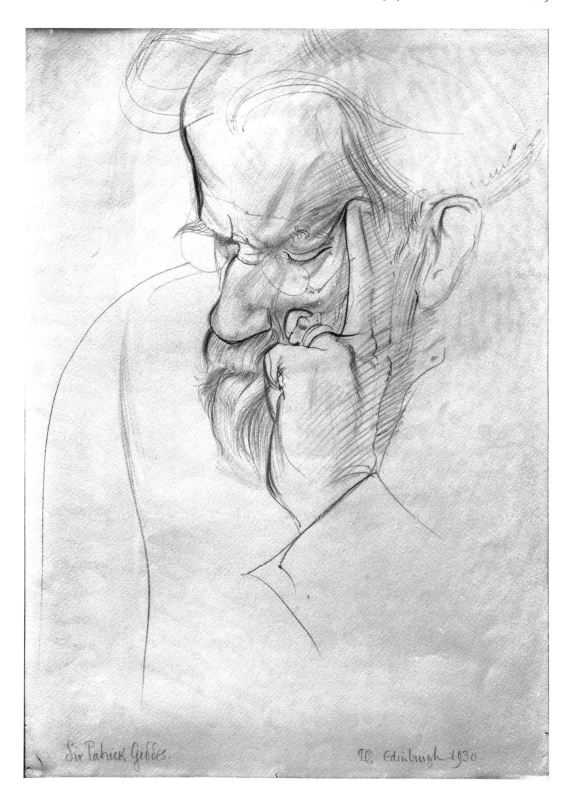

Sir Patrick Geddes.   JD. Edinburgh 1930

to it, and thus maintain that practical indifference to
deplorable conditions which strikes every Continental
visitor, even every American tourist, with an outspoken
astonishment far from flattering to Edinburgh.

In passing one might observe that this observation itself, which
Geddes was far from the first to make, was somewhat flattering to
the Continental visitor and American tourist, either of whom
might have found a similar 'practical indifference' to the 'festering squalor' of slums in their own great cities; even the condition
of the Cowgate compared favourably to that of New York's
Bowery.

Geddes's judgement that there had been 'a disastrous
increase in the social separation of classes who had been in old
Edinburgh so peculiarly mingled' couldn't be challenged, though
his establishment of the Edinburgh Social Union 'to bring
together all those who feel the want of sympathy and fellowship
between different classes' might seem an absurdly ineffective
palliative even to non-Marxists.

Geddes had some practical achievements to his credit,
however. In particular he may be held to have instigated a revival
of interest in the Old Town. He hoped to convert it into 'a
collegiate Street and city comparable with the magnificent High
Street of Oxford and its noble surroundings'. He bought Shorts
Observatory on the corner of Ramsay Street and converted it into
the Outlook Tower. He intended that this should be used to
encourage public discussion of the future of the city; it has
become a tourist attraction. He persuaded the University to buy
old lands in the Lawnmarket and convert them into student
residences. That was a beginning, recently taken further. Geddes
would be gratified to think how much of the Old Town is now
occupied in this way. He built a group of flats himself, in Ramsay
Gardens, intended as a model of Scottish vernacular urban
architecture. They have been admired as such, and it is no doubt
my own lack of architectural knowledge that has led me to think
that they have a rather English look to them.

Geddes was influenced by the Arts and Crafts movement. So
were two architects, Sir Robert Rowand Anderson and his pupil
Sir Robert Lorimer, though they diverted it into a distinctively

Ramsay Garden from the
north

traditional Scottish form. They took their inspiration from the
houses built for seventeenth-century lairds, which were one
stage away from the old fortified house. One consequence was an
efflorescence of crafts in Edinburgh, since this architecture
required skilled stonemasons, wood carvers, iron workers, glass
makers, tapestry weavers and carpenters. Lorimer's masterpiece
would not be built till after the First World War, for it was the
National War Memorial in Edinburgh Castle, but in 1911 he
created a work scarcely inferior: the Chapel of the Knights of the
Thistle in St Giles.

There were other attempts to revive Scottish culture and
rescue it from the sentimentality of the Kailyard and paintings of
stags and Highland cattle. In the middle of the nineteenth
century Edinburgh had produced a number of outstanding
painters, the finest of them being Orchardson, masterly in his

The Chapel of the Knights of the Thistle, St Giles Cathedral by Sir Robert Lorimer

painting of material and in his evocation of mood. But now the most interesting work was being done in the west. In 1907, however, John Buchan, who had recently become a director of the publishing firm Nelson, which had its offices and printing works in the Old Dalkeith Road below Salisbury Crags, established a new magazine called the *Scottish Review*. Buchan, the son of a Free Kirk minister, brought up in Glasgow and the Borders, a graduate of Glasgow University and Brasenose College, Oxford, was determined to eschew the parochialism which disfigured Scottish literary culture. He had contributed to the *Yellow Book* while at Oxford (and incidentally edited a collection of Bacon's *Essays* when he was only seventeen and a first-year student at Glasgow); subsequently he had served under Lord Milner in the reconstruction of South Africa after the Boer War, before being called to the English bar. He had contributed regularly to the *Spectator*, already published half a dozen books and was just thirty-two. It was his intention, he told Lord Rosebery, that the *Review* should 'deal fully with all interests, literary, political and social, with something Scottish in the point of view. We want to make it the centre of a Scottish school of letters such as Edinburgh had a hundred years ago.' The Edinburgh Buchan found himself in was not however Jeffrey's or Blackwood's. The magazine lasted less than two years. A good many other people have since started reviews with the same high intentions as Buchan, and failed as completely. Geddes's Scots renascence was an aspiration rather than a reality.

A young man who would seize that phrase and try to make it his own arrived in Edinburgh in 1908 to train as a teacher at the Broughton Junior Student centre. He was sixteen, his name was Christopher Murray Grieve (though he would later be better known by his alias Hugh MacDiarmid), he came from the small town of Langholm (despite which he was implacably hostile to the Kailyard), this was his first experience of a city, and he did not like it, partly, as he somewhat pretentiously said, because 'of the fact that Cain the murderer was the first city-builder'. Grieve spent five years in Edinburgh, as a student and then as a reporter on the *Edinburgh Evening Dispatch*, and naturally made no mark on it at that time. But his experience is interesting on account of

Hugh MacDiarmid
(Christopher Murray Grieve)
by Robert Heriot Westwater,
1962

what it tells of the intellectual undercurrent, however little impression that made generally either. He was already a Socialist and a regular attendant at the Lothian Road Church Literary and Debating Society. He read Orage's *New Age* and was fascinated by Nietzsche, the first English translation of *Beyond Good and Evil* actually being published in Edinburgh in 1907 under the imprint of the Good European Society, the Darien Press. Socialism and Nietzsche – even Edinburgh was not immune to the forces that would form the new century, or, as MacDiarmid put it many years later:

> The healthy creative force will break through
> – Even in Edinburgh – and good, human things grow,
> Protecting and justifying faith
> In regeneration to a free and noble life
> When labour shall be a thing
> Of honour, valour and heroism
> And 'civilization' no longer like Edinburgh
>   On a Sabbath morning,
> Stagnant and foul with the rigid peace
> Of an all-tolerating frigid soul.

Most Edinburgh people would not of course have recognised that as a description of their condition, with which, what Grieve-MacDiarmid denounced as 'the scum of swinish filth of bourgeois society', they were naturally quite contented.

Sport of one kind or another now played an increasingly important part in the lives of the citizens. Golf of course had long been popular. Charles I had (as we have seen) played the game on Leith Links and so had James VII when Duke of York with a tailor as his partner in a foursome. The oldest golf club in the world is the Honourable Company of Edinburgh Golfers, now established at Muirfield, but at the date of their foundation (1744, ten years earlier than the Royal & Ancient at St Andrews) also playing on the links at Leith. The links at Bruntsfield on what used to be the Burgh Muir date from at least the seventeenth century. By 1900 the growing popularity of the sport meant that Edinburgh was ringed with golf courses.

Professional football commanded the allegiance of the working class. Heart of Midlothian and Hibernian divided the

Mortonhall Golf Club, c. 1892

Heart of Midlothian v Hibernian
Cup Final
at Logie Green, 1896

city, partly on geographical, partly on religious, lines. Sectarianism was not as strong as in Glasgow or Liverpool; nevertheless Hibs drew their support from the Irish immigrants in Leith and Leith Walk and Hearts were firmly Protestant. In time the geographical division between the east and west end of the city became more important in determining allegiance. Even so, one can still hear Hearts supporters apply the adjective 'Fenian' to their rivals. Enthusiasm for football went beyond the working class in Scotland long before it did so in England, for football could already claim to be the Scottish national game. In a memoir of his son Henry Dundas, killed in France in 1918 while serving as a captain in the Scots Guards, R. N. Dundas, a Writer to the Signet, wrote, 'Scottish League football and the prowess of Bobby Walker, Jimmy Quinn and their successors were matters of even greater moment to him all through his boyhood than the *personalia* of English County Cricket and test matches.' If the comparison seems odd, it should be explained that the young Dundas, a cousin of Bob Boothby, was an Etonian. In France, his father adds, 'many an uncomfortable hour was whiled away in discussions with his platoon about the rival merits of "Hairts" and "Hibs" and "Celtic" and "Rangers".'

In general, however, the middle classes were more devoted to rugby, this being the game of all the Edinburgh fee-paying schools. Rivalry between them was fierce, and the years before 1914 were the heyday of the Former Pupils' Clubs, Edinburgh Academicals, Watsonians, and Heriot's FP's regularly producing between them at least half the Scottish International XV, with the boarding schools Fettes, Loretto and Merchiston also nurturing many future international caps. These included the Fettesian K. G. Macleod who, having won twelve international caps and dropped a goal in a great victory over South Africa, retired from the game at the age of twenty-one, in deference to his father's fears that he might incur permanent injury. He later played cricket for Lancashire and football for Manchester City. International matches were played at the Daniel Stewart's ground at Inverleith, and attracted large crowds.

If Glasgow boasted of being the 'Second City in the Empire' Edinburgh retained its vestigial glory as Scotland's ancient capital. This was recognised by a visit from George V and Queen Mary in 1911, the year after the king's accession. They stayed at Holyrood for three nights, and the visit made a great impression. James Bone, in a delightful book, *The Perambulator in Edinburgh* (1926), gives a vivid account:

The Scottish XV before the Scotland v England Rugby International, 1894

> The state of things in Holyrood . . . was a not unfaithful reconstruction of Holyrood life in its old royal days. So, too, were the terms on which George V and Queen Mary lived here with the poorest folk of the Scottish capital hiving only a stone's throw from the Palace . . . 'The rabble was at the Palace doors', the most authentically mediaeval touch of all . . . This contrast between a modern Court at Holyrood and the simple labouring folk of the precinct haunted all the ceremonies, overshadowing them it seemed, like the bare linear hills that frown down from the other side upon the little palace, almost touching its walls . . .

The royal visit was a probe into every part of Edinburgh's economy, and every turn proved more clearly the singular nature of this city. There were moments when it wore the aspect of the capital of Prince Otto's country.* The nocturnal dispersal at Holyrood was one such moment. Another was in the endless procession of carriages – many of them open carriages – extending from the Scott Monument to Holyrood, filled with flowers and ladies, jewelled and arrayed, driving down in the clear northern twilight to the ancient palace lying under the hills. Edinburgh that night was indeed the capital of faerie. It was not in the least like the scene in the Mall on a Drawing Room day. The life of the city went on but the procession was linked to it by the coming and going of pedestrian friends paying their court as the carriages waited on the hill. Another moment was the passage of the Sovereigns to St Giles and the Castle. The poor in these historic dwellings had hung their table cloths and rugs out of the windows, as people still do in Italian cities on a *festa*, and had brought out their chairs and tables on to the pavement and made their own grandstands, while barefooted boys danced everywhere they shouldn't, and the whole scene had a mediaeval inclusiveness one had never witnessed elsewhere in royal progresses.

The Royal garden party at Holyrood provided what Bone calls 'the most characteristic mood of all'.

That venerable and aristocratic corps, the Royal Bodyguard of Scottish Archers, with its five dukes and twenty noblemen in their dark green uniform, flat Scots bonnet and eagle plume, were drawn up for review in Holyrood grounds, and a few hundred people were gathered on a knoll of the hill overlooking the gardens. At a part of the ceremony, the archers, following their ancient custom, sang together the psalm 'I to the hills will lift mine eyes' to the wailing tune of 'French', and the crowd sitting on the hill, rising like guillemots to the sound, joined in the singing, so that the psalm sounded faintly into the Canongate and stole round the hill to awaken the covenanting echoes of Haddo's Hole.

* *Prince Otto*, a novel by Stevenson.

A moment, characteristic of Edinburgh, when past and present became as one, even though the singing of the psalm was no ancient custom, if only because there had been so few occasions since the metrical version was composed that the Royal Body-guard had mustered before their sovereign at Holyrood. Yet at that instant when the poor people of the Old Town lifted their voices in unison with the Archers, it must have seemed like a reconciliation of all the diverse and warring elements in Scottish history, and an affirmation of the essential rightness, even sanctity, of the union. At that moment exclusive Edinburgh briefly recaptured its integrity, and included all its citizens, from Senators of the College of Justice to the wretched of the Canongate and the Cowgate, in a unity of sentiment.

It was 1911. In three years that unity was to be tested as never before. The Empire which had cemented the United Kingdom was on trial. Before the Armistice sounded on 11 November 1918, some of those barefoot boys who had danced everywhere they shouldn't would be killed in the mud of Flanders, drowned in the North Sea or the Atlantic, dead of fever in the camps around Salonika (where Christopher Grieve was serving in the RAMC). The roll of honour in the War Memorial in the Castle lists the names of the dead. Young Henry Dundas wrote to his parents on 24 September, three days before he was killed: 'I had tea yesterday with the 7th HLI who are next to us – in the Lowland Division. Very good, and more typically Scotch than anything you've ever seen. Little sturdy men with tammies and Harry Lauder faces. It did me good to see them.'

The day after his death, his soldier servant, signing himself J. McIntosh, told Mrs Dundas, 'The bagpipes, which he loved so well, played the "Land o' the Leal" when he was laid to rest.' Eleven years later, H. V. Morton wrote of Lorimer's master-work:

> Grief locks the English heart, but it opens the Scottish. The Celt has a genius for the glorification of sorrow. All his sweetest songs are sad; all his finest music is sad; all his greatest poetry springs from tragedy . . . That is why Scotland has built the greatest war memorial in the world . . . The Flowers o' the Forest have all turned to stone.

*The Scottish National War
Memorial
by Sir Robert Lorimer*

The National Shrine does nothing to glorify war, but it echoes the epitaph of Thermopylae:

> Go, tell the Spartans, thou that passeth by,
> That here obedient to their laws we lie.

And that was as true of the barefoot boys of the Canongate as of those reared in comfort like Henry Dundas. It is good, from time to time, to stand for some moments in reverent silence in the National Shrine.

13

Between the Wars

Between the wars there were many who feared that Edinburgh was losing its individuality. It remained a singularly beautiful city, but what was now being built had nothing distinctive about it. Indeed, as bungalows spread out towards the Forth and up Corstorphine Hill and Liberton Brae, no one coming upon one of those streets of neat little dwellings would have been surprised if he had been assured that he was in some other town, even in England. And the same was true of the more ambitious buildings. The Maybury Road-house, for instance, on the Glasgow Road, was a handsome example of Art Deco style, but it might equally well have been found in the Home Counties. Cinemas were perhaps the buildings most completely of the times, but they were distinctively of the times, not of Edinburgh.

For some Edinburgh's loss of character went deeper. Edwin Muir for one thought it impossible to look at Edinburgh 'without being conscious of a visible crack in historical continuity'. Of course, he conceded, the city itself was still splendidly there; the Old Town still reared proudly on its hill; the New Town still spoke of a classical confidence; but, for him, this existed in the past. The town which people actually lived in was 'as cosmopolitan as the cinema'.

Muir is not perhaps the best guide. Admittedly a man of genius, possessed of an unusual penetration, which, although expressed in a very different tone, yet contrives to recall Carlyle, he had too something of Carlyle's weakness: he always saw things at an odd angle, perhaps because his first question was framed in a subjective, rather than objective, manner. Consequently, with both Muir and Carlyle, one thinks that the picture, while a true one, is too partial to be completely convincing. Few other people, for instance, have, I suppose, remarked on the intensity of 'floating sexual desire' which 'fills the main thoroughfare and flows into all the adjacent pockets and back-waters: the tea-rooms, restaurants and cinema lounges'. It is an observation which would have amazed, and then either offended or amused, the ladies of Morningside who descended to Princes Street for shopping and afternoon tea.

Muir was not, however, alone in thinking that Edinburgh had become anglicised. The painter J. D. Fergusson refused to settle in Edinburgh when he returned from France at the beginning of the Second World War, on the grounds that the capital had become a mere suburb of London. The Glasgow playwright James Bridie (O. H. Mavor) inveighed from the west against the decadence of Edinburgh. Once it had been a literary centre, or at least a centre of ferocious literary criticism, but there was no literature in Edinburgh now, no art, no theatre. 'The high places of the city are full of Watsonians,' he added, referring to the former pupils of the most thoroughly respectable and conventional of the great Edinburgh schools. Had he looked a little ahead, he might have remarked that when Watson's produced a politician, it was David Maxwell Fyfe, the most narrow-minded Home Secretary of the last fifty years.

Bridie had no time for the lawyers of his day either – 'a queasy, shabby lot', unworthy of their predecessors – 'whales and porpoises who used to wallow in seas of port and claret'. All this was rumbustious stuff, not without an element of truth, but exaggerated in Bridie's best flyting style. A judge who wallowed in port and claret in 1930 or so would have offended more than the prim inhabitants of the capital's most refined districts.

Edinburgh in reality remained a city of extremes. It was certainly respectable. Nothing showed this more clearly than a murder case in 1926, though the principal characters in the case, a mother and her eighteen-year-old son, were recent arrivals in the city.

Mrs Merrett, a widow, had taken a flat in Buckingham Terrace, so that her son Donald could attend Edinburgh Univer-

sity. Buckingham Terrace, shielded from the traffic of the
Queensferry Road by a row of trees and a secondary access road,
breathes an atmosphere of gentility even today. There is no street
life, and there are no shops. Built around the middle of the
nineteenth century, these houses, substantial and commodious,
were already being converted into flats which attracted people
like Mrs Merrett, or the respectably retired, or well-to-do
spinsters. There they indulged in bridge, tea parties and the
gentle gossip that delights in tracing family connections and
speculates about neighbours and acquaintances. Nowhere in
Edinburgh was more respectable, and it was this which was to
lead to what was almost certainly a miscarriage of justice.

The boy Donald was not an enthusiastic student, preferring
to spend his afternoons and evenings at an establishment in
Picardy Place at the top of Leith Walk which went by the name of
the Dunedin Palais de Danse. Ballroom dancing was the fashion
among the young and the Edinburgh *Evening News* carried
advertisements for seven or eight *palais* on its front page, but the
Dunedin was perfectly reputable. Indeed the widow of a celebrated novelist remembers being taken there and bought her first
glass of sherry by an admirer who would later be a QC. The
Dunedin's advertisement declared that 'Special Thé Dansant
Tickets may be had on entrance and will include a Dainty Tea in
the popular Cafe Rouge'.

Dancing partners were provided by the management. Not
necessarily tarts, they were doubtless more tarty than the girls
whom the parents of the young men who frequented the
Dunedin would have approved. Donald Merrett became
attached to one and formed the habit of booking her out and
taking her for rides on his motor bike. All this was expensive, he
had little money and so he took to forging his mother's name on
cheques. Since her financial affairs were complicated it was some
time before this was discovered, but at last it *was* discovered and
Donald was in difficulties.

What happened then, or rather how it happened, was never
made clear, but the result was that Mrs Merrett was found shot at
her writing table. Donald told the maid she had shot herself, and
this story was repeated to the police. They accepted it, making

only a perfunctory investigation; the reason for their lack of zeal was simply that they couldn't suppose that anything criminal could happen in such a respectable setting. Eventually, when the full story of Donald's conduct was revealed, suspicions were aroused and he was charged with his mother's murder. But the evidence of the experts was (as usual) conflicting, his background told in his favour, and the charge of murder was found 'not proven', though he was sent down for twelve months for forgery. He was consigned to the new prison of Saughton on the outskirts of the city; the great chronicler of Edinburgh crime, William Roughead, described it with some exaggeration as 'a sort of penal garden-city, affording in its humane and hygienic regime the advantages of a rest-cure, a criminous nursing-home, and combining agreeably punishment with amusement', not a judgement with which many of its inmates over the years would perhaps concur. There can be little doubt, however, that if Mrs Merrett had been lodged in the Canongate or Cowgate, then young Donald's story would have been more sceptically received.

But fewer and fewer people lived in the Old Town, for the City Council had embarked on an energetic policy of clearances. The City Architect Ebenezer Macrae was responsible for ambitious housing schemes on the fringes of the city: at Saughton itself, at Piershill, Craigmillar, Niddrie and Silverknowes. The quality of this council housing was often superior to that of the bungalows into which new entrants to the middle classes were flocking. The intentions were of the very best. The estates were spacious and the style of architecture deliberately and intelligently in the Scottish vernacular style, or if not quite in the style, at least paying tribute to it. And yet there was something depressing about them. There was grass for the children to play on, but no pubs for their fathers to visit. There were few shops, and those inadequate. Shopping and work both involved the residents in lengthy bus journeys. But the inhabitants of these schemes were carefully selected from among the deserving poor, and though many who did not live in them sneered and deplored the whole enterprise, there is no reason to suppose that the residents did not find living conditions a vast improvement on the squalor they had left behind. Unfortunately, as the respectable were moved out, the Old Town deteriorated still more rapidly, though the clearances did allow the upper part of the Royal Mile (the Lawnmarket and the High Street) to be renovated, and the architect Robert Hurd also undertook the restoration of Acheson House in the Canongate.

Restoration indeed was in vogue, for there were many who were conscious of the need for Edinburgh to revitalise itself, and this consciousness found expression in civic renewal. The Cockburn Association, one of the first preservation societies in the world, had been founded as long ago as 1875, and in 1936 a body with wider aims came into being. This was the Saltire Society, dedicated to the preservation and enrichment of Scottish culture. It aimed to encourage the development of 'a new Scotland with a vigorous intellectual life, drawing on the past for inspiration to new advances in art, learning and the graces of life'. Its list of original members included Muir, Compton Mackenzie, Eric Linklater, the film-maker John Grierson, the painter D. Y. Cameron, Walter Elliot (Secretary of State for Scotland 1936–8) and Kurt Hahn, the founder of Gordonstoun. None of these was an Edinburgh man, but no doubt the writer Alasdair Alpin MacGregor was mistaken in his assertion that, with a few exceptions, 'the people of Edinburgh neither know nor care a great deal about Edinburgh's stories past'. Such sweeping statements are usually wrong, and the Saltire Society never lacked for Edinburgh members, even if many of the citizens found amusement in the best reductive Edinburgh style in the antics of those who pushed themselves to the fore.

The Saltire itself was the fruit of the self-styled Scottish Renaissance. This had been brought into being, almost single-handed by Hugh MacDiarmid, though the Edinburgh bourgeoisie found his attempts to revive the Scots language more risible than persuasive. He had supporters in the city, though; the poet Helen Cruickshank, a civil servant in the National Insurance Office, made her Corstorphine home a salon for the literati, and MacDiarmid called her the 'catalyst of the Scottish Renaissance. In 1927 she became the first secretary of the Scottish branch of the international writers' organisation PEN, which held its annual conference in Edinburgh in 1934, a foretaste, if nothing more, of developments after the Second World War. Another of MacDiarmid's supporters was William Power, a Glasgow man who moved to Morningside in 1932, the author of one of the best essays on Scottish culture, *Literature and Oatmeal*. Power evolved a grandiose scheme for the renovation of Edinburgh, proposing that the Royal Mile should become a living museum, inhabited by writers and artists. The Canongate was to be 'a literary and artistic faubourg', Edinburgh's Left Bank.

The Renaissance at least encouraged Linklater to set his novel *Magnus Merriman* (the best of his pre-war books) partly in Edinburgh, and its ebullient humour, vivid characterisation, stopping not far short of caricature, caught something vital in the city to which his fellow-Orcadian Muir was blind. Linklater found a gusto in the city which less charitable visitors thought dead.

Literary nationalism led naturally to political nationalism. Both the Liberals and Labour had proposed Home Rule, and a number of bills had been introduced over the years in the House of Commons, but none was ever passed, and in 1928 the National Party of Scotland was formed, though in Glasgow rather than Edinburgh. Four years later this coalesced with the Scottish Party to form the Scottish National Party, and from that time at least dreams of Edinburgh's restoration to the status of a genuine capital were more powerfully dreamed, if never realised. Most of the leading figures of the Renaissance were active in the nationalist movement, but before the war it remained an enthusiasm of a small number of literati and eccentrics.

Edinburgh's own local politics had a nastier tinge. Though the city had not known the deep sectarian divisions of Glasgow, there was nevertheless a considerable resentment of the Roman Catholic minority. To some extent this was quickened by the Irish Troubles after the First World War, which made many Scots apprehensive. In 1923, for instance, the General Assembly of the Church of Scotland approved a report entitled *The Menace of the Irish race to our Scottish Nationality*. This called for 'means to be found to preserve Scotland and the Scottish race and to secure in future generations the traditions, ideals and faith of a great

No. 4   Get the other Three.

THE BIBLE SAYS . . .

CORMACK SAYS . . .

BURNS WROTE:

"Man to man the world o'er shall brothers be an' a' that."

Be a Burns Man

Vote Labour

people, unspoiled and inviolate'. The nationalist intellectual George Malcolm Thomson predicted that if Irish penetration was allowed to continue unchecked, religious and racial riots could not be prevented. When the respectable spoke like this, it is not surprising, given the temper of the time and the example of Fascism on the Continent, that feelings were violent among the less prosperous. They reached a head during the Depression years, and a leader was found in Edinburgh.

John Cormack (1894–1978) was the son of a Baptist lay preacher. He was born in Edinburgh and served in the First World War, then in Ireland during the Troubles. On demobilisation he joined the Scottish Protestant League and soon showed a talent for inflammatory public speaking. A member of the Orange order, in 1933 he founded the Protestant Action Society. He attacked the priest of St Peter's, Morningside, Canon John Gray, accusing him of keeping a mistress for more than twenty years. The attack was misguided, and speaks of ignorance. Gray in his youth had been a friend of Oscar Wilde and, in the mistaken opinion of some, the model for Dorian Gray. St Peter's had been built, and given to the diocese of Edinburgh, on condition that Gray was transferred there from St Patrick's in the Cowgate, by his rich lifelong friend and former lover Mark André Raffalovich.

Cormack was elected for North Leith to the Corporation in 1934, and demanded the repeal of the 1918 Education Act (which gave state support to Roman Catholic schools) and the removal of Roman Catholics from the armed forces, neither conceivably a matter for the City Council. The following year a Roman Catholic Eucharist Congress was held in Edinburgh, and Cormack drummed up a mob in protest. The police put its number at 10,000 and buses carrying Catholic schoolchildren were stoned. At this point Cormack demanded that all Catholics be expelled from Scotland. In 1936 he was charged, fined and briefly imprisoned for organising a riot when the well-known priest Father Ronald Knox came to Edinburgh and broadcast on the BBC. The same year Protestant Action won nine seats on the council and 30 per cent of the vote in the city. This was evidence of a certain turbulence and of an intolerance which the respect-

Caricature of John Cormack: Labour Party Election leaflet, 1937, attacking the Protestant Action Society

able classes preferred to ignore. But it fizzled out. Protestant
Action split in 1937, Cormack lost his seat and though he was
returned for South Leith the following year and remained a
councillor till 1962, his day as a demagogue of some influence was
over even before the war.

Far more important was the transfer to Edinburgh of the
Scottish Office. 'It was,' writes Michael Fry, 'more than administrative reform. It had immense symbolic value, making
Edinburgh once again a seat of government, truly a capital rather
than just the headquarters of the Kirk and judiciary.' It was also
an effort to raise the standing of a department which had been in
a state of some confusion. The chief mover in this was Walter
Elliot, the most influential Tory between the wars. Elliot had no
time for nationalism, but he was a fervent Scottish patriot. St
Andrew's House was itself the development of an earlier plan to
collect together the various boards, quangoes and offices with
responsibility for managing Scottish affairs. It was Elliot who
insisted it must be the headquarters of the Secretary of State.

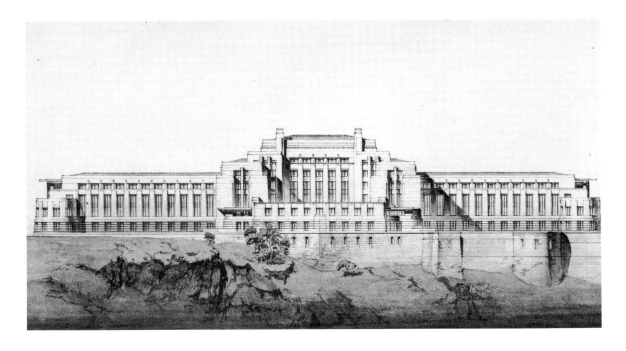

The design of the building provoked the usual controversy,   *St Andrew's House*
even Queen Mary chipping in with the request (or demand) that   (south elevation)

it should be 'something noble and worthy of the site', which was on the flank of Calton Hill, something moreover, she made clear, which would not spoil the view from Holyrood, which she apparently prized, though she was seldom there. The design was entrusted to Thomas Tait, and the result was a building of some dignity, in a sub-Fascist style of architecture; sub-Stalinist too if it came to that. Few can ever have thought it beautiful, but few have found it positively offensive; and for a long time that was as much as anyone could hope could be said for a new building on a prominent site in Edinburgh. It was opened in mid-September 1939, just in time for the war.

It meant little to most of the inhabitants of the city; the senior civil servants were reticent, largely invisible. Socially, they never challenged the supremacy of the lawyers or the academics. There were few who could even name the Permanent Under-Secretary of State, the high heid yin of St Andrew's House. However, as the decades passed, the reality of administrative devolution would become for many an additional reason for demanding the return of a Parliament to Edinburgh. As John Smith, the future leader of the Labour Party, observed in 1980: 'To have one's legislative body four hundred miles away is the perfect recipe for mandarin government – a description that fits the Scottish Office only too well.' Even some of the mandarins, when retired and freed from the responsibility of office, would eventually be found to agree.

In the 1930s, however, other things mattered more to the ordinary citizen. For the middle class it was a comfortable time. The young, as Muriel Spark has made clear in her autobiography, found it then, as always, an exciting city, with its contrasts, its whiff of danger behind the tranquillity. Another young writer, Robert Taubman, then a pupil at the Royal High School (still on Calton Hill gazing at the rising St Andrew's House), found it 'a stronghold of antique establishments' – a good term, still applicable. The professional population never seemed to him 'just a piece of class structure'. It had too distinctive a character, was too rooted in a past which somehow – no one could be sure in what manner or why – still contrived to breathe. It was a city which did not willingly reveal its secrets. Life was lived largely behind closed doors. It was no surprise to a young man or woman walking along Queen Street to learn that in No. 52, almost a hundred years earlier, in 1847, the future Sir James Simpson, and his assistants Dr Duncan and Dr Keith, had experimented with chloroform and 'were all "under the table" in a minute or two'. It was just the sort of thing that ought to happen in that street of dead windows which Ruskin had so disliked.

Looking back on her days at James Gillespie's Girls' School, Muriel Spark recalled that pivotal word 'nevertheless'. She saw in memory 'the lips of tough elderly women in musquash coats taking tea at MacVittie's, enunciating this word of final justification'. Justification was still in the air of Edinburgh. It was no longer a political capital, might never be again; nevertheless. She was surely right in thinking that in her time the society of Edinburgh regarded what went on down there in London, government and administration, Parliament and politicians, as 'just a little bit ridiculous'. When, as a Member of Parliament, Bob Boothby would return to his parents' house, looking the worse for wear after a night on the London train, his mother kept an eye on his whisky intake. He might be an MP, but in Edinburgh he had better behave himself.

In many respects Edinburgh was fortunate between the wars. Not being an industrial city, it suffered less from the depression than many places. In 1933 one of the worst years of the decade, when Hitler came to power and unemployment was at its peak all over Western Europe and the United States, Edinburgh opened its new open-air swimming pool designed to the Olympic standard, at Portobello. It could accommodate 6,000 spectators, and had lockers for almost 1,300 bathers, not to mention a restaurant, snack bar, tea gardens, rest rooms and a wave machine. At the other end of the city, on Corstorphine Hill, where Jeffrey of the *Edinburgh Review* had had his Horatian villa, there were now the Zoological Gardens, opened the year before the First World War, attainable by tram and already famous for their penguins and their breeding programme. The zoo, the cinema, the tea rooms, the *palais de danse*: all spoke of a certain softening of Edinburgh's mood. All contributed to the attractions the city could offer visitors. Glaswegians defined the difference

Portobello Swimming Pool in the 1930s
photograph by Frank Wilson

between the two cities, so close geographically, so distinct in their ethos, in a joke that has stood the passing of time sufficiently well to be retold. The caller at a Glasgow residence, they said, would be received with the invitation to 'come away in and have your tea'. The Edinburgh greeting would be different: 'You'll have had your tea.'

Perhaps the joke was on Glasgow, suggesting that the Edinburgh visitor would be too polite to put his or her hostess to the trouble of making tea. The institution of tea is dead, and yet the joke is still held to identify a distinction between the warmth which Glaswegians love to ascribe to themselves, and the frigidity which they claim to find in the Edinburgh character. Certainly there is a now traditional reserve to it. But not all incomers found the city unaccommodating; my own mother, coming from rural Aberdeenshire, to study at the College of Domestic Arts in Atholl Place (itself famous for having produced a cookery book which won the admiration of Elizabeth David) found Edinburgh friendly, eminently civilised, a delightful place to be young in. Of that cookery book, written by the Principal of the College, Florence Jack, Mrs David wrote, 'There is useful detail and the directions are very clear.' Precision of that sort was dear to the Edinburgh temperament.

A better distinction between Edinburgh and Glasgow was offered by the English travel-writer H. V. Morton:

> Glasgow plays the part of Chicago to Edinburgh's Boston.
> Glasgow is a city of the glad hand and the smack on the
> back; Edinburgh is a city of silence until birth or brains
> open the social circle. In Glasgow a man is innocent until
> he is found guilty; in Edinburgh a man is guilty until he is
> found innocent. Glasgow is willing to believe the best of
> an unknown quantity; Edinburgh, like all aristocracies,
> the worst.

There is something in this, with one proviso: that Edinburgh cherishes its known villains and eccentrics more fondly than Glasgow does its.

Morton's understanding went deeper. He saw that it was all to some extent a pose. 'Edinburgh pretends to be more precious than she is; Glasgow pretends to be more material than she is.'

The North British Hotel: arrival hall in the inter-war years

Then he went to the heart of it, though his next distinction is one that many contemporary Scots, especially Glaswegians, find it hard to accept. The real difference, he thought, is that Glasgow is 'cosmopolitan' – the easternmost city of the United States, as I have put it myself, forever re-inventing itself, while Edinburgh, he thought, is Scottish. So much for Muir and the fears of the literati.

Even today a foreigner can come to Glasgow and find it recognisable, himself quickly at home: 'Glasgow is like Naples,' a Neapolitan once told me; but Edinburgh is always itself, *sui generis*, though in dissatisfied moments I have sometimes found in it something of the repellent and reticent self-assurance and self-sufficiency of Florence, my least favourite Italian city.

But one of its curiosities is its ability to come to accept, and take as essential to itself, something new which it has initially rejected. This is a strange peculiarity for a place that is so conscious of its history, and so driven to trade on it. A good example is furnished by the history of the two great railway hotels built at either end of Princes Street: the North British at Waverley and the Caledonian at the long-since departed Princes Street Station. Both were at first deplored. The Caley, it was said, had been conceived in Glasgow, reared there and then shunted along the railway line. Who could ever tolerate a building in that red stone in Edinburgh? As for the North British (grotesquely renamed the New Balmoral) George Scott-Moncrieff denounced it as 'a colossus of nastiness, a giant wart'. Now a proposal to demolish either would arouse equal fury. Like the National Disgrace on Calton Hill, they have become well-loved landmarks, affectionately regarded, and not only by those whose first memory of arrival in Edinburgh has been a kipper or finnan haddie there, after a rough night on the London sleeper.

14

Painting

Medieval Scotland had its painters and carvers, but few are known and little of their work survives, partly on account of the Presbyterian Kirk's distrust of the decorative arts. The influence of the Kirk and the departure of the court in 1603 prevented the emergence of a Scottish version of the baroque. The royal courts, the Catholic Church and the great nobility were characteristic patrons of art in Europe; all were lacking in Scotland. So were the great merchants, who served as patrons to Dutch painters. Some small stimulus was given in Charles II's reign; even so, it was a Dutchman, James de Witt, of more perseverance than talent, who was contracted to paint and deliver within two years of signing the contract, for a salary of £120 per annum, 110 portraits 'in large royall postures' of all the kings – most of them mythical – who had reigned over Scotland from King Fergus the First to King Charles the Second, 'our Gracious Soveraigne'. This could hardly be compared with commissions executed at Versailles, or even Whitehall.

Nevertheless, the art of painting did make some progress, despite all obstacles in that century. There was John Anderson, who flourished from about 1600 to 1649 and is known to have worked at Edinburgh Castle. He had a pupil, George Jamesone, from Aberdeen, who was apprenticed to him in 1612 and became the first master of the art of portrait painting in Scotland. Horace Walpole compared him to Van Dyck, and he is believed to have died a rich man in Edinburgh during the Civil War.

Jamesone had no immediate successor of comparable talent. It is not till the early eighteenth century that we can speak of a

Self-Portrait by James Norie

school of painting in Edinburgh – or indeed Scotland. This centred round the Norie family, originally interior decorators, supplying decorative panels and frames, and painting landscapes for use over doors and between windows, for architects and their clients. James Norie Senior (1684–1757) established the business, with sufficient success for him to be co-opted on to the Town Council. He and his two sons, James and Robert, specialised in creating agreeable pastiches of Italian and Dutch landscapes to complement the works of art which noblemen might bring back from the Grand Tour. The Nories' work was skilful and craftsmanlike, as the panels in Prestonfield House in Edinburgh show. They also took on apprentices, and a number of painters started their career in this way. These included Alexander Runciman (1736–85) who was later sent by Sir John Clerk of Penicuik, a member of one of the great legal families, to study in Rome, on the understanding that on his return he would decorate Penicuik House. Unfortunately his work there, *The Hall of Ossian*, was destroyed by a fire in 1899, but Runciman excelled in Classical landscapes in the manner of Claude Lorrain or his own friend and master Henry Fuseli.

The Nories were also involved in the establishment of the first Painting Academy in Scotland. The Academy of St Luke, founded in 1729, lasted only three years, but its members included the two Allan Ramsays (father and son), William Adam the architect, the portrait painter John Alexander, the engraver Richard Cooper, and Roderick Chalmers, who combined the trades of house painter and heraldic artist.

The younger Allan Ramsay was Scotland's first indisputably great painter, combining strength and delicacy in an unusual manner. Much of his work – even portraits of Scottish noblemen – was in fact executed in his London studio, but he maintained a studio in Edinburgh also and never lost his links with the city; he was, as already noted, one of the founders of the Select Society in 1764. Though he attained his greatest celebrity as court painter to George III, his finest works are not in the Grand Manner which royal portraiture demanded. Duncan Macmillan has suggested that 'Ramsay elevated portraiture to a humane science. His marvellous portrait of David Hume [in the Scottish National

overleaf
Classical Landscape by the Nories in its original setting in Prestonfield House

David Hume
by Allan Ramsay

Portrait Gallery in Queen Street] 'reflects not just the close knowledge of a friend, but the penetration of an equal and kindred intelligence'.

During Ramsay's lifetime Scotland's first enduring art institution was founded in Edinburgh. This was the Trustees' Academy, established by the Board of Trustees for the Encouragement of Manufacturers in Scotland. Its original purpose was to provide instruction and training for pupils following, or intending to follow, one of the decorative trades; and the intention was clearly utilitarian. However, Alexander Runciman, who was the Academy's third Master, and his successor David Allan appear to have been successful in giving it a bias towards their own principal interest, painting.

One of its early pupils was Alexander Nasmyth (1758–1840), who subsequently worked with Ramsay. Nasmyth, born in the Grassmarket, the son of a builder, was to be an influential figure in Edinburgh for more than half a century. He was sent to Italy by his friend and patron, Patrick Miller of Dalswinton, for whom he had made mechanical drawings in connection with Miller's interest in steam navigation. His Italian experience determined him to become a landscape painter; he was influenced by the work of Claude and Jacob More. When he returned to Edinburgh he built himself a house at 47 York Place, where he established a drawing school. He continued to paint Italian landscapes there, working from drawings made in Italy, but he was soon also working on Scottish subjects. In Nasmyth, as in Runciman, we can see two styles, or rather two modes of feeling, coming together and finding new expression. On the one hand there was the romanticised Classicism drawing its original inspiration from Poussin's paintings of the Roman Campagna; on the other, the new Romantic feeling for Scotland, which found its first expression in Macpherson's *Ossian*, and which was to be fully developed by Sir Walter Scott. In 1821 sixteen drawings by Nasmyth, depicting Scottish views associated with the Waverley novels, were engraved by W. H. Lizars, another graduate of the Trustees' Academy.

Like the Nories', Nasmyth's was a family business, and like them he was versatile, working also as a landscape gardener for noble patrons such as the Duke of Argyll and the Marquis of Breadalbane. His four daughters also taught at the drawing school, from which Nasmyth would take his pupils on sketching trips to Arthur's Seat, Duddingston Loch, Roslin and Craigmillar Castles, and even the Pentlands – wherever, in the vicinity of Edinburgh, the picturesque could be found. Both his sons, Patrick and James, were distinguished painters, though James also worked successfully as an engineer, inventing the steam hammer. Alexander Nasmyth designed the charming St Bernard's Well by the Water of Leith.

Nasmyth was an almost exact contemporary of Henry Raeburn (1756–1823), who, with Ramsay, is Scotland's greatest portrait painter. Raeburn was born in Stockbridge, the son of a mill owner, and educated at George Heriot's. He was first apprenticed to an Edinburgh goldsmith, James Gilliland, and began painting miniatures while still an apprentice. Marriage to a rich widow gave him freedom to study and travel, and after working briefly in Sir Joshua Reynolds's London studio, he made the obligatory visit to Rome in 1784. He returned to Edinburgh two years later, and it was to be his base for most of the rest of his life. Like Nasmyth, he established himself in York Place (No. 32), where he had not only a studio, but also a gallery which he lent for exhibitions by other painters. He made his reputation with his painting of Sir John and Lady Clerk of Penicuik (1792). It was exhibited at the Royal Academy in London and praised for its 'boldness of touch and strength of effect'.

Boldness and strength were indeed Raeburn's characteristics, in contrast to the delicacy of which Ramsay had been capable. He worked, unusually, without preliminary drawings, concentrating from the first on the face, from which, he said, 'nothing ought to divert the eye'. Stevenson, in his essay *On Some Portraits by Raeburn*, said that his genius was to be found in his ability 'to plunge at once through all the constraint and embarrassment of the sitter and present the face, clear, open and intelligent as at the most disengaged moments'. Raeburn paints character, as well as features; this is one reason why he was most successful with those sitters who had lived long enough to let experience mark them. He was fortunate perhaps that his

Edinburgh, and Scottish, clients do not seem to have sought flattery at his hand.

He painted all the legal luminaries and the cream of Edinburgh society, being especially successful with mature women. His series of portraits of Highland clan chiefs were the visual equivalent of *The Lady of the Lake* and *Waverley*; they marked not only an important development in Romantic painting but were also part of the process of reconciliation between Lowland and Gaelic Scotland. It was appropriate that he twice painted Scott himself, in 1808 and 1822. The earlier work, which now hangs at Abbotsford, is the often reproduced painting of Scott with the bull-terrier Camp and a deerhound. At this first session painter and sitter failed to establish friendly relations; the painting's power is not softened by affection.

The success of painters such as Raeburn and Nasmyth depended on the existence by that time of a considerable prosperity in Edinburgh and the country in general, though even so Raeburn's price for a portrait was only a third of that charged by his most celebrated English rival, Lawrence. Raeburn also belonged, thoroughly and unquestioningly, to his own time. He was the fine fruit of the second age of the Scottish Enlightenment; there is no reproach or satirical intent in his work. He shares the moral outlook of his sitters and measures them against the standards which they had in common. He paints them from within an agreed consensus. It is Raeburn's assurance and solidarity with his sitters that gives his work its authority. His is Establishment painting at its finest.

Three years after Raeburn's death, the Scottish Academy was established. (It received the charter which entitled it to use the prefix 'Royal' in 1838.) Founded in emulation of London's Royal Academy, of which Sir Joshua Reynolds had been the first president in 1768, it was also a statement of the self-esteem and confidence to which Scottish painting had attained. Its objects were clear and simple:

1. To hold an Annual Exhibition open to all artists of merit.
2. As funds increase, to open an Academy where the Fine

Lord Newton
by Sir Henry Raeburn

Arts may be regularly cultivated and students admitted free
of expense.
3. To open a Library devoted to the Fine Arts.
4. As all artists are not equally successful and as some
acquire neither fame nor fortune but, after many years of
painful study, at a time of life when it is too late to think of
other pursuits, find themselves destitute, to provide
charitable funds.
5. And lastly, to add Grace to this Society, admit Honorary
Members eminent by their talents and attainments.

The Academy took over the Royal Institution at the bottom of the
Mound, and Playfair created the handsome building which we
know today; it remains the property of the RSA despite the
jealous and acquisitive eye reputedly cast on it by the Trustees of
the National Galleries. The Trustees' Academy also moved into
the building, provoking a long-running quarrel between the two
institutions, not resolved till 1858 when the RSA took over the
Life School, leaving the Trustees' Academy to teach only 'the
Antique'. In effect this meant that the Trustees' Academy was
responsible only for elementary instruction, and it gradually
withered away, leaving the RSA in the ascendant, a position it
held until the Edinburgh College of Art was founded in 1909.

By the time the Academy was founded – in the same year that
Playfair also embarked on the construction of the National
Monument on Calton Hill – Scotland and Edinburgh were well
established as the Ideal of the Romantic and Picturesque. The
Edinburgh Review, in an article probably written by Jeffrey
himself, temporarily discarded its Whig sobriety and the scepticism which Jeffrey had brought to contemplation of Scott's
medievalism in *Marmion*, to declare:

> It is the peculiar boast of Edinburgh, the circumstance on
> which its marvellous beauty so essentially depends, that
> its architecture is its landscape; that nature has done
> everything, has laid every foundation, and disposed of
> every line of its rocks and its hills, as if she had designed
> it for the display of architecture . . .

*The Sculpture Gallery of the
Royal Scottish Academy* before
conversion, c. 1908

Or, indeed, for the delight of Romantic painters. It was no surprise, therefore, that English artists flocked north, in response to the feelings excited by Scott's poems and novels, ready to depict these scenes for the pleasure of the growing middle-class public who, if they could not themselves afford a Turner or a Landseer (both of whom visited Scott at Abbotsford, and painted him or his demesne), could content themselves with engravings of the works of these Romantic masters, or with the oils or watercolours produced by their numerous disciples.

But there was another, domestic style of painting, truthful at its best, sentimental rather than picturesque when it fell short of that level, a style more influenced by the Dutch school than by the pseudo-Classical Italian landscapes. The master of this genre was David Wilkie, a Fifer, who had an enormous influence on other artists. He worked little in Edinburgh, and his best paintings were of rural and domestic scenes, but in forming a style in which the daily life of ordinary people could be satisfactorily depicted in a realistic, homorous and sympathetic manner, he created an image of the other Scotland, couthy and Presbyterian rather than romantic and picturesque; and this was perhaps nearer the reality of experience for most folk. A contemporary working in the same manner was Walter Geikie (1783–1837), a native of Edinburgh and a deaf mute, who had a keen and tender eye for Edinburgh's poor and deprived.

Scott was a friend and admirer of Wilkie, whose portrait of the novelist and his family at Abbotsford was condemned by London critics as 'a vulgar group' unworthy of 'an elegant poet'. But Scott knew the value of Wilkie's work: there is a remarkable passage in *The Antiquary*, in which Scott begins by remarking that 'in the inside of the cottage was a scene which our Wilkie alone could have painted, with that exquisite feeling of nature that characterises his enchanting productions', and then proceeds to describe what is in effect a Wilkie painting drawn only in words.

Wilkie succeeded Raeburn as King's Limner in Scotland, and was commissioned to paint a record, unfortunately never completed, of George IV's visit to Edinburgh. Indeed, soon after this appointment, Wilkie had what appears to have been a nervous breakdown; when he recovered, he attempted, with less success, paintings in the academic style, intended principally for the London market. He also tried a Scottish Historical style, as in his unfinished *John Knox Preaching*, and this too owed much to the interest in Scottish history of which the Waverley novels were at once an example and a cause.

George IV's Entrance at Holyrood by David Wilkie, 1828

Sir William Allan (1782–1850), another product of the Trustees' Academy, worked successfully in this style. He returned to Edinburgh about the time of Waterloo, after ten years in Russia, where he had painted Tartar horsemen and Circassian maidens. Encouraged by Scott, he now painted *The Murder of Rizzio* and *The Murder of Archbishop Sharpe* on Magus Moor in Fife, this latter being vividly described by Scott in *Old Mortality*. Allan, a friend also of Wilkie, made genre paintings, such as *The Penny Wedding*, in his manner; and when Scott's last publisher, Robert Cadell, brought out the *magnum opus* edition of the Waverley novels in the last years of Scott's life, it was to Allan that he turned for illustrations.

This style of Scottish Historical painting was to be continued by other former pupils of the Trustees' Academy, who had been taught there by Allan. James Drummond (1816–77), born in the Canongate (actually in the house popularly believed to have belonged to John Knox), established his reputation with a large-scale painting of *The Porteous Mob*, which again drew on an event and scene described by Scott, this time in *The Heart of Midlothian*. Following Wilkie and Geikie, he also recorded many of the old streets and wynds of Edinburgh. Drummond, like Scott, had antiquarian interests and a great knowledge of arms and costume, so that his work is in some ways a visual companion to the detailed descriptions of such matters in the Waverley novels.

Sir William Allan's successor as headmaster of the Trustees' Academy in 1844 was another Historical painter, Thomas Duncan, who specialised in scenes from the Jacobite Risings; his last painting, *George Wishart Administering the Sacrament*, not only makes reference to Wilkie's unfinished painting of John Knox, but, since Wishart, burnt for heresy in St Andrews in 1546, was the morning star of the Reformation in Scotland, it was also a statement of contemporary historical significance, the Disruption having occurred in 1843, two years before Duncan's death.

The Disruption, appealing deeply to the historical as well as the religious imagination, since it called up memories of the Covenanters, was recorded by David Octavius Hill (1802–70), painter and pioneer of photography, first in a series of calotypes (an early form of photograph) and then in a huge painting depicting the exodus from St Andrew's Kirk led by Chalmers; Hill worked on this for almost twenty years, and the references it displays to David's *Oath of the Tennis Court* (1790) acknowledge the revolutionary significance of the breakaway of the Free Church.

Throughout this period painting derived much of its vitality from the close connection it maintained with the other arts, especially literature, and literature's dramatic presentation of history. Its relationship with architecture was also close; Robert Adam's drawings of the ruins of the palace of the Emperor Diocletian at Spalatro had influenced two generations of painters, as well as architects and interior designers. There was,

Dr David Welsh (one of the leaders of the Disruption): calotype by David Octavius Hill and Robert Adamson

moreover, before the camera invaded this territory, a healthy market for drawings and engravings of famous buildings and beauty spots, which few painters disdained to satisfy. Most remarkably, in little more than half a century, painters, largely based in Edinburgh, had created a distinctively national style of art, moving away from an often delightful, but inevitably derivative, rendering of Classical or pseudo-Classical Italian landscapes to a self-confident realisation of the charms and beauties of their own country, buttressed by the conviction that scenes from Scottish history were as valid a subject for the painter as those from Classical mythology, and might be painted with a greater sincerity, while appealing more deeply to the public.

This confidence found public expression in the foundation of the National Gallery of Scotland. It was not the first such scheme. Back in 1780 the eleventh Earl of Buchan, gifted, egocentric and foolish, had conceived the idea of founding what, somewhat off-puttingly, he had called a 'Temple of Caledonian Virtue', bringing together a collection of objects and paintings which might be thought to illustrate that theme. Buchan was one of the founder members of the Society of Antiquaries of Scotland, and his collection was the embryo from which the National Museum of Antiquities eventually developed, finding a home in the 1880s building given to the city by John Ritchie Findlay, proprietor of *The Scotsman*, to house the National Portrait Gallery.

The National Gallery itself had no such stumbling be-ginning. The foundation stone was laid by the Prince Consort in 1850. The architect was Playfair, who devised a handsome building in the same style as his Royal Scottish Academy, behind which it stands. (It was necessary to remove first a popular attraction known as Wombwell's Menagerie.) The gallery was opened in 1859, two years after Playfair's death. Subsequent extensions (the most recent taking its lower level surprisingly near the railway line that passes beneath it) have not destroyed its intimate charm. It remains excellently stocked and must be one of the most agreeable and rewarding national galleries in the world. It is just the right size, and native works by Ramsay, Raeburn, Wilkie, Runciman, Allan, Orchardson and others gain from being hung beside masterpieces from Italy, France, Spain, the Netherlands and England.

Yet there is a sense in which the building of the National Gallery marks the end of the heroic age of painting in Edinburgh, and even Scotland. Good painters were still emerging from the schools and academies, but from the middle of the century there is a discernible slackening of purpose and intensity. It was perhaps inevitable: the zest had gone out of Scottish intellectual life. Henceforward artists – painters and writers especially –

could choose to please a large, undemanding, but easily un-
settled, public, which wanted above all the reassurance afforded
by the familiar – Highland landscapes and a view of history that
was increasingly sentimental and divorced from things as they
had truly been. Artists could rebel against this, but that almost
always meant either a retreat into some private world or a turning
to foreign models, which they might then strive to re-integrate
into what was left of a vigorous Scottish tradition.

Some of the best painters of the mid-century, like Sir Joseph
Noel Paton, Sir William Fettes Douglas and William Bell Scott, all
pupils of the accomplished Robert Scott Lauder at the Trustees'
Academy, were influenced by the English Pre-Raphaelite group,
whose own rebellion was lukewarm and transmitted to the
Scottish group in diluted form. This easily degenerated into
whimsical prettiness, as in Noel Paton's *Quarrel between Oberon
and Titania* (National Gallery). Another and more accomplished
pupil of Lauder's was William Quilter Orchardson (1832–1907), a
masterly painter of detail, whose characteristic canvases combine
historical and genre painting in a refined, even dandyish,
manner. But Orchardson early removed to London, and did most
of his work there. So did his friend John Pettie, one of the most
successful of Victorian historical painters.

Duncan Macmillan judges that though there was much
first-class painting in this period, 'creative leadership for
Scotland in the visual arts was no longer to be found within
Scotland. There was no longer that essential imaginative drive on
which great art depends. There is much individuality of manner
in the painting, but no sense anywhere of a particular individual
pursuing a compelling personal vision that dictates its own
forms.' He carries this criticism down at least as far as the First
World War, observing also that there was no equivalent in
painting to Charles Rennie Mackintosh, and that it was perhaps
significant that Mackintosh, 'like R. L. Stevenson, used his sense
of a native Scots tradition as the frame of reference for his
response to more exotic influences'.

There were exceptions to this general stricture. William
McTaggart (1835–1910), another of Robert Scott Lauder's pupils,
pursued an individual vision with great pertinacity and success.

Even more individual, though less recognised, was James Pryde (1866–1941). The son of the headmaster of Queen Street Ladies College, Pryde worked mostly in London, but his work includes a series of remarkable paintings inspired by Queen Mary's bed in

Lumber: a Silhouette by James Pryde

Holyroodhouse. An exhibition at the Edinburgh Festival in 1992 did much to restore Pryde's reputation.

Nevertheless Duncan Macmillan's criticism largely holds good. 'Agreeable but ordinary' is the common verdict on most late nineteenth-century painting, at least in Edinburgh. (There was rather more vitality in Glasgow.) The establishment of the Edinburgh College of Art in 1909 may be taken as an attempt to foster a renaissance. It inherited the old tradition of the Trustees' Academy of teaching by distinguished artists and introduced a new rigour, while encouraging a sense of adventure, which bore fruit between the wars. The foundation of the 1922 Group, by graduates of the college, including W. G. Gillies and William

W. G. Gillies at work on a landscape

MacTaggart (grandson of the Victorian McTaggart), marked the beginning of the renewed ascendancy of Edinburgh in Scottish painting. The group was soon joined by Anne Redpath and John Maxwell; all these were painters who had absorbed foreign, especially French, influences and transmuted them into something characteristically Scottish. The Edinburgh School, as they came to be called, were little concerned with theoretical arguments about Modernism; they eschewed abstraction, while at the same time incorporating some of the painterly qualities suggested by it. Their style was further developed after the war by painters like Robin Philipson and James Cumming, whose work is nicely poised between the abstract and the figurative, while drawing also on very old Scottish motifs to be found in Celtic art. This Edinburgh School dominated the RSA for more than half a century, several of its members being president.

Yet for all this, and despite the wealth of galleries in Edinburgh – the most notable recent addition being the Scottish National Gallery of Modern Art, in what used to be John Watson's School above the Water of Leith – and despite the stimulus given by the Festival and the proliferation of privately owned commercial galleries, notable among which are Aitken Dott's The Scottish Gallery, now more than 175 years old, and the adventurous, often experimental, 369 Gallery; despite this, it cannot be claimed that painting has recaptured the position of centrality which it enjoyed during the Enlightenment. It does not matter as it did then, even though in those days the public to which it appealed was smaller.

This paradox is to be explained partly by the nature of modern mass society, devoted to consumerism, partly by the sense that Scottish intellectual life has no characteristic impetus of its own, but exists as a paler copy of life being lived more intensely elsewhere. Perhaps also Edinburgh, in love with its idea of its own past, discouraged the new in painting as in other activities.

15

Post-War

Edinburgh suffered little during the war, no worse than sleepy English provincial cities, just a few bombs in Leith docks. Of course it endured the privations common to the whole country: shortage of food, shortage of warmth, shortage even of drink. Individuals, however, suffered grievously, chief among them those who lost family and friends in the enforced surrender of the 51st Highland Division at St Valéry, a disaster which Eric Linklater compared in its effects to Flodden itself. But other Scottish units not in that division got away at Dunkirk, the first battalion of Edinburgh's own regiment, The Royal Scots, distinguishing themselves in the defence of Le Paradis on 27 May 1940 and suffering heavy casualties.

Two years later, on 23 June 1942, the leader of the Free French, General de Gaulle, visited Edinburgh and made a speech in which he alluded to the gallantry of the Scottish regiments in the Battle of France, and spoke in warm and noble tones of the Auld Alliance:

> In our old alliance there was more than a common policy, more than marriages and fighting deeds. There were not only the Stuarts, the Queens of France and Scotland, Kennedy, Berwick, Macdonald and the glorious *Garde Écossaise*. There were also a thousand ties of spirit and soul. How could we forget the mutual influence of French and Scottish poets, or the influence of men like Hume on our philosophy? How could we fail to recognise what is common to the Presbyterian Church of Scotland and the doctrines of Calvin? How could we hide the influence which the great Walter Scott has exercised over the

Self-Portrait by
George Jamesone

*Self-Portrait with
John Brown* by
Alexander Runciman

Princes Street during the Building of the Royal Institution by Alexander Nasmyth, early 1820s

The Porteous Mob by James Drummond

Opposite *Interior of the National Gallery*, c. 1870s (anon.)

Noontide, Jovie's Neuk by William MacTaggart.
A bay in East Lothian with a distant view of Edinburgh

Sir Compton Mackenzie
by Robert Heriot Westwater,
1962

Muriel Spark by Alexander Moffat

The Thrie Estaites: scene from
the 1991 revival of Robert Kemp's
1948 adaptation performed
in the Assembly Hall

Edinburgh Festival Theatre
(model),
Law & Dunbar-Nasmith,
Architects

receptive mind of French youth? How could we ignore all
the exchange of ideas, feelings, customs and even words so
frequent between our two peoples joined by such a natural
friendship, a friendship of which a visit to Edinburgh
affords such ample proof?

A few years after the war, a Francophone, if Belgian-born,
novelist, Georges Simenon, visited Edinburgh. Standing on the
castle rampart, he pointed to a building in Princes Street and
asked his companion, the writer Moray McLaren, what it was.
'Oh,' said McLaren, 'that's the monument to Sir Walter Scott.'
'What,' Simenon replied, 'they erected such a monument to a
novelist?' He paused for thought. 'Well, why not?' he continued.
'After all, he invented all of us.'

He was quite right. Scott was the true father of the European
novel. And his comment was appropriate in another sense, for in
the miserable and ravaged Europe of the years after the war,
Edinburgh lit a new beacon in the cause of culture, while culture,
in the form of high art, may also be said to have given new life to
Edinburgh. It is no exaggeration to claim that the inauguration of
the first Edinburgh International Festival in 1947 was of at least as
great symbolic importance as the publication of *Waverley* in 1814.

Yet the Festival might very easily have alighted elsewhere. It
was the brainchild first of Sir Rudolf Bing, the conductor of the
Glyndebourne Opera (and later of the Metropolitan Opera in
New York). He was convinced that such a celebration of art was
necessary as a restatement of the European ideal and the human
spirit after the obscenity of Nazism. He expressed this opinion in
conversation in a London club to Henry Harvey Wood who, by a
happy chance, was the British Council representative in
Edinburgh. He responded with enthusiasm and then talked to Sir
John Falconer, the Lord Provost of Edinburgh. Falconer, with an
imagination and intelligence which perhaps none of his predecessors in office had displayed since Drummond fathered the
New Town, seized the opportunity; and so Edinburgh became
the home of what is still the greatest and most comprehensive
Arts Festival in the world.

Perhaps the most moving occasion of that first Festival was
the reunion of the great conductor and pianist Bruno Walter with

*Air-raid shelter, East Princes
Street Gardens*

his beloved Vienna Philharmonic Orchestra, from which he had been separated since he was driven into exile when Hitler's stormtroopers goose-stepped into Vienna. That reunion, perfect in symbolism and human sympathy, was the complete expression of what Bing, Harvey Wood and Falconer had set themselves to achieve. They were three men to whom the world, and Edinburgh, owe more than could ever be repaid.

The second Festival achieved a reconciliation, less moving, less dramatic, but, in the context of the cultural history of Edinburgh and Scotland, almost equally remarkable and momentous. It had been decided to revive Sir David Lyndsay's play, *The Thrie Estaitis*, never performed since the Reformation. The director was to be Tyrone Guthrie, Irishman of genius, but himself the great-grandson of the Scottish divine Dr Thomas Guthrie who had founded the Ragged Schools and whose statue stands on the Gardens side of Princes Street. No suitable theatre existed. No suitable hall could be found. Even the skating rink at Murrayfield was inspected, and judged inadequate. Then at last Robert Kemp, playwright, pillar of the little Gateway Theatre in Leith Walk, and BBC producer, said to Guthrie, 'in the tone', Guthrie recalled, 'of one who hated to admit something unpleasant, "There is the Assembly Hall . . ." '

It was a bold, even impious, suggestion. The Assembly Hall, smoke-stained, dark and gloomy on the Mound, was the annual meeting place of the Church of Scotland. The statue of John Knox loomed forbiddingly in its courtyard. For centuries the black-gowned ministers had denounced the theatre as an invitation to iniquity, even though the author of Scotland's first ambitious verse tragedy, *Douglas*, had been a minister, the Reverend John Home. But now the Kirk's attitude had softened, or grown more civilised. Guthrie was granted the use of the Assembly Hall, and *The Thrie Estaitis* became the sensational success of the Festival, supplying a necessary Scottish content, sometimes in later years thought to be insufficient.

The Assembly Hall has ever since been a Festival venue, and one where some of the greatest performances have been staged. These would include a patriotic verse drama, *The Wallace*, by the much loved poet Sydney Goodsir Smith. The enthusiastic reception it got might be evidence of the audience's national fervour rather than their critical sense, but, if so, this too recalled the first performance of *Douglas* when one excited citizen called out in triumph, 'Whaur's your Wullie Shakespeare noo?' That hadn't stopped the zealots of the day from attacking Home, who had to surrender the ministry of his parish, while the Kirk's Session Court also prosecuted ministers who had attended the theatrical performance. But now all was changed. The Kirk was at its highest level at least reconciled to Art, even approving. The use of the Assembly Hall as a theatre during the Festival symbolised that the split in the Scottish psyche created by the Reformation had at last been healed.

Of course not all Festivals were successful, not all productions escaped the condemnation of the unco' guid, not all City Councillors approved of this encouragement of culture, not all the citizens were happy to see Edinburgh become for three weeks every summer the setting for a celebration that drew visitors from all parts of the world. Some of the staider residents preferred to withdraw for the duration to Highland hotels or the golf courses of Fife. They missed much but were not greatly missed themselves.

The Fringe soon started, as amateur and semi-professional companies hired halls for themselves and put on their own productions; but in the early days there was no danger that the Fringe would appear to swamp the Festival itself. It was no more than an agreeable adjunct. One of the charms of the early Festivals was their intimacy. Edinburgh still suffered from extremely restrictive licensing laws. It was impossible legally to get a drink after an evening performance, except in a hotel where you were a resident, or in the Festival Club itself, created not only to provide a meeting place but to circumvent the restrictions on the sale of alcohol; for it was very reasonably felt that visitors from European cities, where the consumption of liquor was not considered moral at nine o'clock and immoral at ten, would find this Edinburgh (and British) distinction quaint but uncomfortable. So the Festival Club established itself in the Assembly Rooms in George Street where Scott had admitted to his authorship of the Waverley novels; and one of its charms was that the ordinary theatre- or concert-goer might find himself or herself rubbing shoulders with the Greats in whose performance they had been delighting half an hour earlier. In time, as the licensing laws were liberalised, the Festival Club withered. This was natural, but something was lost.

There were other restrictions in the grim post-war years. There were few restaurants of any quality. Even as late as 1961 the *Good Food Guide* could find only five to recommend, and one of them was Cadbury's Chocolate House in Princes Street, described as 'an espresso bar that serves chocolate instead of coffee'. It was a favourite with the young during the school holidays. Unaccountably missing from the list of recommendations was the Café Royal Oyster Bar, with its magnificent late Victorian stained glass. The most popular restaurant, still

The Festival Club in the Assembly Rooms, 1956

regretted by all who remember it, was L'Apéritif in Frederick Street. Not only was the food admirable, but it always seemed a place of endless possibility. One night a well-known novelist, dining on lobster with a celebrated advocate, turned to a lady not previously encountered and as an opening gambit said, 'Madam, will you open your legs for me tonight?' She declined the invitation or request; nevertheless, in the best Edinburgh fashion, she remained unphased.

There were pubs in Leith Walk, of course, where the request, if put more plainly, would have met with easy acceptance. Some such were celebrated by Sydney Goodsir Smith in his poem-sequence *Under the Eildon Tree*:

> I got her i' the Black Bull
> (The Black Bull o Norroway)
> Gin I mynd richt, in Leith Street,
> Doun the stair at the corner forenent
> The Fun Fair and Museum of Monstrosities,
> The Tyke-faced Loun, the Cunyiar's Den
> And siclike . . .

Sydney Goodsir Smith was one of a group of poets who used to congregate in the Rose Street bars, especially Milne's and the Abbotsford, and who revived something of the spirit of eighteenth-century Edinburgh while at the same time creating a Soho or Fitzrovia of the North. The centre of the group was MacDiarmid, though he lived in Lanarkshire and his visits to Edinburgh were infrequent. Some wrote in Scots, which MacDiarmid himself had now for the most part abandoned and which was for the time being usually known as Lallans. Smith did so as successfully as any, which in a sense was a surprise, for he had been born in New Zealand, returned to Scotland when his father became Professor of Forensic Medicine at the University of Edinburgh, but then received a conventional upper-middle-class education at Malvern and Oriel College, Oxford. He claimed to have learned Scots from village children during school holidays at Moniave in Dumfriesshire; but though this gave him a feel for the rhythms of the language, the vocabulary and aureate style of his best poetry was drawn from his predecessors in the fifteenth and sixteenth centuries, especially Dunbar. At his best he has

Sydney Goodsir Smith by Denis Peploe

opposite
Milne's Bar: etching by John Bellany

something of the exuberance and virtuosity of Dunbar, and parts
of *Under the Eildon Tree* celebrate twentieth-century Edinburgh in
a manner that bridges the centuries to join hands with Dunbar.

A more natural colloquial Scots was written by Robert
Garioch, whose affinities were with the sad eighteenth-century
genius Robert Fergusson rather than with Dunbar. Garioch
commented with wry, downbeat meiosis on the Festival itself, on
manifestations of civic pomposity and the University's Philistine
redevelopment of George Square and its environs, in a poem
called *A Wee Local Scandal*:

> . . . the Hume toure – it hits ye in the ee,
> young muckle black rectangle in the air,
> a graund sicht frae the meedies, man; it fair
> obliterates Arthur's Seat; nae word of a lee . . .

But how, he wondered, had they the nerve to name it after David
Hume, who had been denied a professorship by the same
University on account of his religious views?

It is in his poem *At Robert Fergusson's Grave, October 1962* that
Garioch most movingly united Edinburgh's past and present:

> Canongait kirkyaird in the failing year
> is auld and grey, the wee roseirs are bare,
> five gulls leam white agin the dirty air:
> why are they here? There's naething for them here.
>
> Why are we here oursels? We gaither near
> The grave. Fergussons mainly, quite a fair
> turn-out, respectfu, ill at ease, we stare
> at daith – there's an address – I canna hear.
>
> Aweill, we staund bareheidit in the haar,
> murning a man that gaed back til the pool
> twa-hunner year afore our time. The glaur
>
> that haps his banes glowres back. Strang, present dool
> ruggs at my hairt. Lichlie this gin ye daur:
> here Robert Burns knelt and kissed the mool.

I know only one other sonnet in Scots to match it: Mark
Alexander Boyd's sixteenth-century 'Twa loves I hae . . .', so
admired by Ezra Pound.

Not all the poets wrote in Scots, even a modified Scots such as Garioch used here. The master of those who preferred English was, and is, Norman McCaig, a poet of wit, sensibility and laconic rhetorical skill, his heart and mind divided between Edinburgh and the Western Highlands. The same division gave a nervous strength to Hector McIvor, Gaelic poet, broadcaster and inspirer of the young in his capacity as master in charge of English at the Royal High School. When he died, too young himself, Karl Millar, Cockburn's biographer, put together a book of essays in his honour, called *Memoirs of a Modern Scotland*.

And not all the poets were good. The English poet George Barker, after enduring a night of alcoholic bravado, composed a squib, *Scottish Bards and an English Reviewer*, which began:

> And in the Abbotsford
> Like gabbing asses
> They scale the heights
> Of Ben-Parnassus . . .

If the poets gave a certain tone to the city, richer perhaps in memory than in contemporary experience, it was a tone then largely unrecognised by the mass of Edinburgh's citizens, who went about their daily business indifferent to bards and reviewers alike. Moreover, if poets flourished, publishing did not. Edinburgh's long boast of being the second publishing centre in Britain was ever more threadbare, as old-established firms like Nelson's and Oliver and Boyd lost their independence, and Chambers withdrew from general publishing to concentrate on reference books. Blackwood's too was in decline, though Compton Mackenzie, who had established his principal residence at 31 Drummond Square and became the most dignified ornament of Edinburgh's literary life, was to declare in an article written in 1967 to celebrate the 150th birthday of the 'Maga', that 'as long as Blackwood's Magazine continued to appear, I had no fears for Edinburgh's supremacy as a city'. Alas, its fame had long diminished, its circulation was declining and, despite a valiant effort by David Fletcher, the first non-Blackwood to edit the magazine, to breathe fresh life into the institution, it expired in 1980, surviving Mackenzie himself by fewer than ten years.

If there was change and decay in certain aspects of Edinburgh life, change was being resisted and decay arrested in others. A proposal to surrender the city completely to the motor car by driving a motorway through the Meadows found vociferous supporters, fortunately outnumbered by those who could recognise vandalism when it was so barely presented without even a mask. Then the New Town, which in some parts was being threatened with the same physical deterioration that had overcome the Old, and therefore with the social effects that would necessarily follow, was saved. In 1968 the Festival had staged an exhibition, entitled '200 Summers in a City', celebrating the New Town's bicentenary. This led to a survey undertaken by the Edinburgh Architectural Association, which revealed the deterioration of both the social and physical fabric. An international conference was held in the Assembly Rooms in George Street in 1970 and the first result was the establishment of the New Town Conservation Committee. The determination to preserve an urban environment worthy of the ideals which had brought it into being was now clear; and the New Town was protected, restored and revived. The work of this committee offered an example that would be followed by other European cities, and even by Glasgow. In a few years further restoration of the Old Town and its extension on the South Side would follow. Even the academic vandals of the University found themselves checked.

Not everything hideous could be prevented, however. Leith Street, at the top of Leith Walk, was destroyed to create the monstrous St James's Centre and New St Andrew's House. But by and large, Edinburgh suffered less from the zeal for redevelopment characteristic of the 1960s than any other major British city.

There was one important economic development. Edinburgh had been a centre for banking and insurance for a long time: the Bank of Scotland was founded in 1695, the Royal Bank of Scotland in 1727. Some of Britain's greatest insurance companies, such as Scottish Widows and the Life Association of Scotland, had their headquarters in the city. (Scottish Widows incidentally built one of the finest modern buildings in Edinburgh, a smoke-glass structure cunningly echoing the outline of the Salisbury Crags which formed its backcloth.) Now there was a further expansion

Leith Street from the clock tower of the North British Hotel, prior to demolition

of financial enterprise. The first merchant bank was founded in the late 1960s by two enterprising young men, Angus Grossart and Iain Noble. Others followed. Fund managing became an Edinburgh speciality; Charlotte Square took on a new significance, meaning in Edinburgh what the City meant in London. By 1980 it was claimed that Edinburgh controlled or managed the investment of more money than any financial centre in Europe except London and Zurich. In 1982–3 a threat to the growing self-confidence of the financial sector was beaten off, when an attempt by the Hong Kong and Shanghai Bank to absorb the Royal Bank of Scotland was rejected by the Monopolies and Mergers Commission, largely as a result of the weight and number of representations made to the Commission by an extraordinary variety of institutions and individuals in Scotland. A few years later, the principal industrial enterprise with its headquarters in Edinburgh, Scottish and Newcastle brewers, achieved an equally notable success when it repulsed the ambitions of the Australian brewing conglomerate Elders XL.

Edinburgh had its failures, too. It was still reluctant to recognise the extraordinary individual, as the art entrepreneur Richard Demarco had frequent occasion to complain. It had its moments of old-fashioned prudery which more often made the objector seem ridiculous than the thing objected to reprehensible. There was the long-running saga of the opera house, a farce that raised fewer laughs the longer it ran. The heart of the matter was simple. Neither of the two civic theatres, the King's or the Lyceum (though both artistic gems) was suitable for any large-scale opera production; and for the city that boasted itself the home of the finest Arts Festival in the world to be without a theatre in which an international opera or ballet company would not be embarrassed to work seemed ridiculous to more people than the successive Directors of the Festival. But the City Fathers were made of stern stuff. They didn't see why opera companies couldn't adapt, make do and mend. They were convinced that an opera house would be a white elephant forty-nine weeks of the year, not conceiving (apart from the other uses to which it might be put) that the existence of such a theatre might actually foster a demand for opera and ballet. So they hummed and they hawed and they delayed, and at last said they would provide a site and even put up some money, if the government would do the rest, which actually meant the most. But the government would not play ball, and so for many years the famous hole in the ground remained in Castle Terrace – Edinburgh's new disgrace, but less attractive than the old one, since a partly built Greek temple may look an attractive ruin, while a hole in the ground has more comic than visual appeal.

Eventually the matter was resolved. The hole in the ground was filled by a handsome office building designed to attract financiers from Charlotte Square, while a nod to the original intention to devote the site to Art was given by the incorporation of the new Traverse Theatre within it. Meanwhile, the old Empire Theatre on the Bridges, a bingo hall for the last quarter-century, was bought for conversion into, at last, a true opera house, opening in the summer of 1994. (With a somewhat depressing predictability, it has been renamed the Festival Theatre.)

The provision of sporting facilities was approached with a little more confidence. The Commonwealth Games came to Edinburgh in 1970, and a fine swimming pool was built for the occasion below the Salisbury Crags. Meadowbank Stadium was upgraded, a synthetic track laid, and the games were a success. Their second coming sixteen years later was less happy, marred by a boycott by some African countries and financial mismanagement on such a scale that for a time it looked as if the games might not take place – a prospect so shameful that even Robert Maxwell, publisher, financier and crook, was welcomed as a saviour.

In the 1980s the Scottish Rugby Union, which sixty years earlier had shown an enterprise never matched by the Glasgow-based Scottish Football Association by building its own national stadium at Murrayfield, embarked on a programme of redevelopment. When finished it will accommodate more than 60,000 spectators, all seated. The result will be magnificent, but in the opinion of many who have loved the great bowl of the old swelling terracing, it will no longer be Murrayfield. Nevertheless, the enterprise of the SRU has run in parallel with one of the most successful periods of Scottish rugby, during which two Grand Slams have been won, the final deciding match on each occasion

being played in a highly emotional atmosphere at Murrayfield. *The Commonwealth Games, 1970*
The capital's two principal football clubs, Heart of Midlothian
and Hibernian, may look enviously at the achievements of the
SRU, for, after some years of success in the post-war seasons,
both have endured long barren periods and both need to
redevelop their grounds to meet the demands for public safety
advanced in the Taylor report; both lack the financial resources to
do what is necessary, and neither is prepared to collaborate with
the other in a ground-sharing scheme.

The late 1970s was a period of renewed, and unusual, political
excitement in Scotland, as the Labour government engaged on a
timid and tentative scheme to devolve a measure of self-
government. Thomas Hamilton's Royal High School on Calton
Hill was purchased to be the home of the proposed Assembly (the
building was conveniently vacant since the Council had removed   *The Royal High School*
the school to the affluent suburb of Barnton in order to make it   by Thomas Hamilton

less élitist). There was much talk of Edinburgh becoming a 'real' capital again, and the media, especially *The Scotsman* and the BBC, were excited by the prospect of having 'real' politics on their doorstep. Distinguished journalists like Neal Ascherson and Colin Bell were attracted back to Edinburgh, and if at the time of the union the church bells had rung out the tune 'How Can I Be Sad Upon My Wedding Day', there was no question that the prospect of even a semi-divorce could fail to arouse a degree of merriment.

The Eleven SNP MPs, 1974

But the matter was more complicated than it seemed. The Scottish National Party, whose unexpected success in the decidedly peculiar General Election of October 1974 (when it had won eleven seats) talked enthusiastically of 'one more push', even while it derided the inadequacy of Labour's Bill. There was renewed talk of embassies in Edinburgh and of Scotland taking its seat at the United Nations between Saudi Arabia and Senegal. Meanwhile Labour, which had only embarked on its policy of devolution because it was alarmed by the threat offered by the SNP, was itself divided, the MP for West Lothian, Tam Dalyell, heading a group of dissidents opposed to the measure. His tireless reiteration of what was called the 'West Lothian Question' – 'How can I vote on education in Accrington but not in Aramdale, in Burnley but not in Bathgate?' – exposed some of the oddities of the Bill. Other sceptics rallied. The Conservative Party, which had itself proposed devolution only a few years back, was also divided, though it mostly fell into line behind the new party leader Margaret Thatcher, who was opposed to the Bill – and not only because it was a Labour measure. Then, outside the Central Belt, there were doubts throughout the country. Scottish business was especially dubious and mounted and financed a campaign which asserted that 'Scotland is British'. The Bill was seen as an attempt to impose enduring Labour government on Scotland at a time when the party's popularity was declining in the United Kingdom as a whole. The north-east of Scotland declared its unwillingness to be 'ruled by Strathclyde'. The Labour MP for Islington, George Cunningham, himself a Scot, introduced an amendment which required 40 per cent of the whole electorate to vote 'yes' in the promised referendum for the Bill to become law. When the referendum came, the 'yes' vote fell just short of that figure; the Scotland Act was shelved; and then the government fell and Mrs Thatcher became Prime Minister.

The circumstances gave rise to a good deal of bitterness, for the 'yes' vote had achieved a majority of those actually voting in the referendum; however, the indignation was somewhat spurious, since less than two-thirds of the electorate had voted, and, the Cunningham amendment ensuring that abstention was the same as voting 'no', it was impossible to tell how many of those who did not bother to vote were opposed to the Scotland Act, and how many did not care about the thing one way or another. At any rate, there was no devolution and the energy and enthusiasm which the prospect had created seeped away.

Perhaps the real mistake was to have selected the Royal High School building in the shadow of the unfinished National Monument as the home of the New Assembly. In retrospect the symbolism seems trite but undeniable.

Envoi

We began with Carlyle walking to Edinburgh as a young student and being taken almost straight away to Parliament House to catch the flavour of the city and get a sight of its great men. No modern student – not even if his subject is law – is likely to head for Parliament House. Many – indeed, probably most – will pass their whole University career in the city without feeling the need to imitate Carlyle. And yet the courts still sit there, the Senators of the College of Justice still deliver their judgements, advocates still perambulate the Great Hall in conference with their clients, before repairing to the court room or slipping back into the Advocates' Library. It is all more orderly, and tamer, than it was in Carlyle's day, but essentially the same. Parliament House offers the interested visitor confirmation of Edinburgh's capacity for continuity. It is still a city of lawyers, and the continuing independence of Scots law remains the guarantee of Scotland's distinct identity.

In Carlyle's day the week of the General Assembly of the Kirk was the most important in the city's year, for if there was no Parliament, and if much of the law was made anew as a result of the interpretations of the judges, the General Assembly represented the conscience of the nation, visible and undeniable. Many would like to think it still does so; the Kirk's committee that pronounces on public affairs is given the name of 'Church and Nation'. Yet, every decade, the Kirk speaks to, and for, a smaller part of the nation; and though the week when the General Assembly meets attracts attention in the media, Edinburgh is apparently for the most part unaware of the occasion.

The University which Carlyle attended was, before the reform of Oxford and Cambridge some thirty years later, the best in the United Kingdom. It is still distinguished, but there are now three universities in Edinburgh, for it has been joined by Heriot-Watt and Napier. The academic community is much larger, more diverse and less fully integrated in the city. Indeed, Edinburgh in general now gives the impression of being a city of distinct communities with little communication between them.

But this is probably true of most cities. It is only remarkable in Edinburgh because of one's knowledge of the past, of how in the eighteenth century it was a city in which solitude must have been almost impossible. Even so, even with these reservations, it remains an intimate city. You can walk from the lower New Town to the Meadows beyond George Square in a comfortable half an hour, and at most seasons of the year you are likely on such a walk to encounter someone you know. Edinburgh escapes on the whole the inhumanity of the great modern city: the feeling of alienation in a crowd is foreign to it. It is a city on a human scale; even its National Galleries – the Portrait Gallery in Queen Street and the Gallery of Modern Art above the Dean village, as well as Playfair's National Gallery itself at the foot of the Mound – are of a size which is inviting rather than deterrent. In each of them you can hope to see everything currently on display in a single visit, though each has a sufficiently large number of great or profoundly interesting paintings to invite a leisurely return.

Thanks to a mixture of good fortune and civic inertia, it remains a visually exciting city, a place of sudden and dramatic vistas, a place where only the dull of imagination can lose an awareness of its past. The old name, the Athens of the North, is now meaningless, despite the Grecian temples on Calton Hill. The resemblance is rather to old Rome, which offers the same delight to the eye and the historical imagination.

To know Edinburgh you have to walk it, braving the wind. You have to feel it in the nip of a winter morning and the glow of a summer evening. You have to turn off the High Street into the dark wynds and closes, and stand and listen to the voices of the past. You have to sit in the pubs and the gardens of the New Town (for which you will require an invitation from a keyholder). You have to view the Firth from the castle ramparts and from the heights of the Calton Hill. You have to stand in the kirkyard of Greyfriars and attend a service in St Giles. And yes, even now, you have to imitate Carlyle and enter Parliament House, for, unless you do so, you will miss much that has made Edinburgh what it is.

There is a saying about Rome: *una vita non basta*: one life is not enough. I think it applies to Edinburgh also, this city of the picturesque where the mirror reflects a different and darker face.

Index

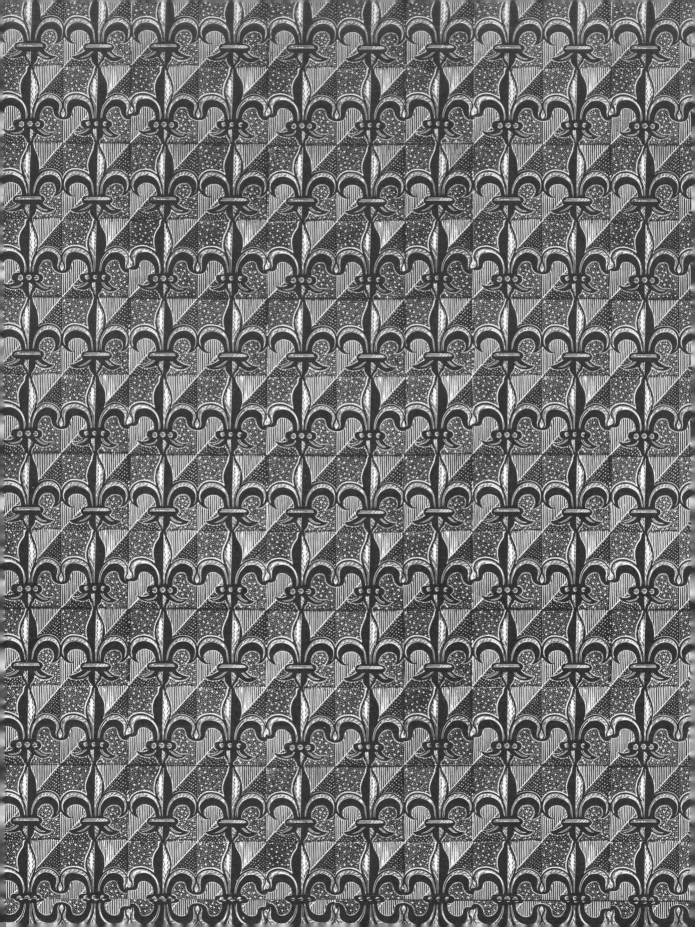